McDougal, Littell
SPELLING

Brown Level

Dolores Boylston Bohen
Assistant Superintendent
Fairfax County Public Schools
Fairfax County, Virginia

Mary Johanna Lincoln Huycke
Elementary Teacher and Reading Specialist
Fairfax County, Virginia

 McDougal, Littell & Company

Evanston, Illinois
New York   Dallas   Sacramento   Raleigh

Objectives

- to teach the spelling of **words** as well as the spelling of sounds
- to stress the recognition of **structural** similarities as well as phonetic similarities
- to strengthen **associative** and **visual memory**
- to reinforce the **three modes of learning:** visual, auditory, and kinesthetic

Organization

Each lesson presents a word list that demonstrates one spelling pattern or generalization. The list is followed by three types of activities:

Practice the Words—three activities that require students to examine and write the words on the spelling list at least twice

Build Word Power—an activity that extends the application of words on the spelling list in a broader language arts context

Reach Out for New Words—two activities in which students work with new words that follow the spelling pattern

CONSULTANTS FOR THIS TEXT

Georgene G. Albert, Teacher, Pine Tree Independent School District, Longview, Texas
Olive L. Engebretson, Teacher, School District of Chetek, Chetek, Wisconsin
Ann B. Hackett, Teacher, Traverse City Area Public Schools, Traverse City, Michigan
David V. Johnson, Curriculum Specialist, Mount Diablo School District, Concord, California
Barbara E. Marthaler, Teacher, Millcreek Township School District, Erie, Pennsylvania
Joanne McDonald, Teacher, Portage Public Schools, Portage, Michigan
Evelyn J. Meredith, Teacher, District 208, Oneida, Illinois
Edith M. Olson, Teacher, Barron School District, Barron, Wisconsin
David E. Prince, Teacher, Irvine Unified School District, Irvine, California
Claire A. Stewart, Teacher, Jefferson Public Schools, Jefferson, Wisconsin
Jacqueline Wadlinger, Teacher, Durham County Schools, Durham, North Carolina
Elsa E. Woods, Principal, Durham County Schools, Durham, North Carolina

Acknowledgments: See page 232

ISBN 0-8123-5420-6

91 92 93 / 15 14 13 12 11 10 9 8 7 6 5 4

Contents

A Writer's Journal

Spelling Is for Writing

Imagine that you are drawing a picture of your friend. You want to show just what your friend looks like. Now imagine that you are writing about that friend. You want to use certain words in your description. But wait! What will happen if you cannot spell any of those words?

You learn to spell in order to write. Writing is something you do often. This book will help you improve both your spelling and your writing. The more you practice both skills, the better speller and writer you will become.

One way to practice writing is to keep a journal. A journal is a notebook where you write your ideas, feelings—anything at all.

Start to keep a journal today. Write in it often. Sometimes you may write a few lines. At other times you may fill several pages. Here are some ways to use your journal.

- Write what you think or feel.
- Remember special times in your life.
- Describe how something looks or sounds.
- Tell about a favorite story or poem.

Spelling and Your Journal

When you write in your journal, you may want to use words you cannot spell. Do not stop writing. Write the words as you think they should be spelled. Later, look up the correct spelling in the dictionary. Keep a personal word list of these words. Then, whenever you need to write them again, just check your list.

Getting Started

If you need an idea for your first journal entry, start with one of these.
1. Today I imagined that . . .
2. You should see the _____ that I saw!

Building a Personal Word List

What Is a Personal Word List?

Your spelling book shows you how to spell many words. It also gives you information about how words in our language are spelled. In this way, the book helps you become a better writer. Sometimes, however, you will need to write a new word that you do not know how to spell. You can put this word on a special list called a personal word list. This is a list of words that *you* want to learn how to spell and use. This list is special because *you* choose the words you want to make your own.

Words for your personal list can come from anywhere—your writing, your reading, or your conversations. You also might discover words for your list in these other places:

- your journal entries
- your other subjects
- stories and poems you write
- newspapers and magazines

How to Keep a Personal Word List

Write your personal words in a special place. This might be in the back of your journal or in a special notebook. Be sure to keep your list handy. That way, you can add words and look at the list easily.

As you collect the words, check them carefully. Notice the kinds of spelling mistakes you make. Think about the words. Do any of them look like words you know how to spell?

Making Words Your Own

Making a word your own means making it one you can use in your writing. You will need to know its meaning and correct spelling. A dictionary can help you. Then you will want to learn to spell the word. The steps on page 7 show one way you might use to learn to spell words.

How to Spell a Word

Each week you will be learning to spell a new list of words. You will also be learning words from your personal list. You will need a system—or strategy—for studying these words. One way to learn to spell a word is explained below. You can use it as you prepare for your weekly spelling test and as you learn to spell words on your personal list.

1. Look at the word.

2. Say the word.

3. Spell the word aloud.

4. Copy the words.

5. Picture the word in your mind.

6. Cover the word and write it.

Check for mistakes.
If you have made a mistake,
repeat steps 1 to 6.

mil<u>e</u>	*mile*
lak<u>e</u>	*lake*
rac<u>e</u>	*race*
plac<u>e</u>	*place*
hos<u>e</u>	*hose*
cag<u>e</u>	*cage*
siz<u>e</u>	*size*
priz<u>e</u>	*prize*
ston<u>e</u>	*stone*
past<u>e</u>	*paste*
sinc<u>e</u>	*since*
onc<u>e</u>	*once*
mor<u>e</u>	*more*
non<u>e</u>	*none*
gon<u>e</u>	*gone*

1. What is the last letter you see in the word **mile**?

2. What is the last letter you hear in the word **mile**?

3. The words in the first column end with a
letter that cannot be heard. What is that letter?

Many words end with a final silent **e**.

A Print the spelling word that fits in the shapes and rhymes with the clue word.

1. space | p | l | a | c | e |

2. size

3. taste

4. pose

5. done

6. store

7. prince

8. bone

9. face

10. file

11. prize

12. rage

13. bake

9

B Find the misspelled word in each group. Then write the word correctly.

1. size
   lake
   plase

2. wonce
   stone
   mile

3. hose
   more
   caje

C Use each clue to find a spelling word that fits the boxes. Write the words.

1. what a winner gets

2. a running contest

3. for watering grass

4. a rock

5. opposite of **less**

6. how big a thing is

7. a long distance

8. not any

9. one time

10. no longer here

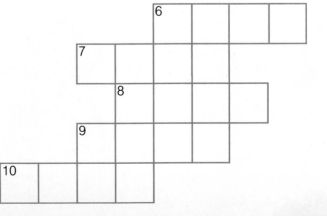

Build Word Power

Writing

Choose a spelling word. Write an acrostic poem about your word.

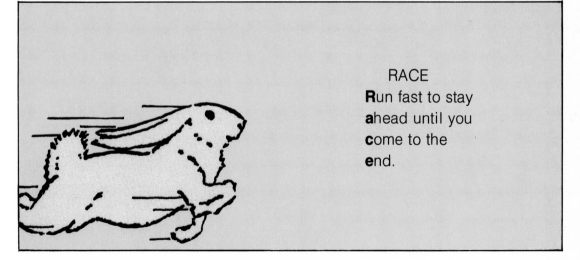

CAGE
Closed inside
a tiger was
growling and
eating his food.

RACE
Run fast to stay
ahead until you
come to the
end.

Let the spelling word be the <u>title</u> of your poem.
Begin each line with a letter of the spelling word.
Start the poem with a capital letter. End it with a period.

Reach Out for New Words

A Find the eight new silent **e** words in this puzzle. Write each word.
Some words may overlap.

Proofreading

B Find each misspelled word. Write it correctly.

1. The tiar is flat. Therefor, we must walk. (2 words)

2. The breeze is blowing smoak at me. (1 word)

3. What is the prise of this flower vaes? (2 words)

b<u>oa</u>t	*boat*
c<u>oa</u>t	*coat*
g<u>oa</u>t	*goat*
fl<u>oa</u>t	*float*
r<u>oa</u>d	*road*
l<u>oa</u>d	*load*
t<u>oa</u>d	*toad*
t<u>oa</u>st	*toast*
<u>oa</u>k	*oak*
s<u>oa</u>k	*soak*
s<u>oa</u>p	*soap*
c<u>oa</u>ch	*coach*
thr<u>oa</u>t	*throat*
c<u>oa</u>st	*coast*
<u>oa</u>ts	*oats*

1. The letters **a**, **e**, **i**, **o**, and **u** are vowels. What two vowels are in each word?
2. Which one of the two vowels do you hear when you say these words?

Some vowels are paired to spell one sound.
Many words are spelled with the vowels **oa**.

boat   goat   road   toad   oak   soap   throat   oats
coat   float   load   toast   soak   coach   coast

Practice the Words

A Use each clue to find a spelling word that fits in the puzzle.

Across
3. person who trains a team
5. browned bread
9. a tree
10. what a truck carries
11. street

Down
1. ship
2. food travels down this
3. long jacket
4. animal with horns
5. like a frog
6. you wash with it
7. to keep in water
8. to lie on top of water

B Answer each question with spelling words.

1. Which five words have the letter **s**?

2. Which three words have the letter **d**?

3. Which four-letter words end with the letter **t**?

C Unscramble each group of letters to make a spelling word.

1. posa

2. loaft

3. otca

4. accho

5. tago

6. otba

7. osta

8. rattoh

9. staot

10. oask

11. dloa

12. ako

13. dota

14. droa

15. scoat

boat   goat   road   toad   oak   soap   throat   oats
coat   float   load   toast   soak   coach   coast

Build Word Power

Writing

Write some silly sentences. Use two or more **oa** words in each sentence. Circle those words. Use as many different spelling words as you can. Remember to start each sentence with a capital letter and end it with a period.

The (toad) ate (toast) under the (oak) tree.

16

Reach Out for New Words

A The three words in each group below belong together.
Write the new **oa** word that goes with each word group.

1. wood, oil, coal, ___

2. bake, fry, broil, ___

3. juice, milk, tea, ___

4. earn, spend, save, ___

5. brag, gloat, cheer, ___

6. moan, cry, sob, ___

B Find the misspelled word in each group. Then write the word
correctly.

1. coat	**2.** road	**3.** goat
baost	coco	load
toast	boat	laon
oak	groan	float
4. coach	**5.** raost	**6.** soap
boast	toad	float
soak	soap	groane
charcole	toast	coach

Words spelled with ou

out	*out*
about	*about*
count	*count*
found	*found*
ground	*ground*
round	*round*
around	*around*
sound	*sound*
loud	*loud*
cloud	*cloud*
mouth	*mouth*
south	*south*
hour	*hour*
house	*house*
mouse	*mouse*

What pair of vowels do you see in every word?

Many words are spelled with the vowels **ou**.

Practice the Words

A Write the spelling words that complete these sentences.

1. Birds fly ___ for the winter.

2. A marching band plays very ___ music.

3. I hear the ___ of an airplane flying.

4. Dale wrote a story ___ horses.

5. My little brother can ___ from one to ten.

6. The sun was hidden behind a ___.

7. A baseball is ___, but a football is not.

8. I burned my ___ on some hot soup.

9. Kim took a sweater ___ of the drawer.

10. In the mile race, the girls ran ___ the track four times.

11. I ___ a dollar on the ___.

12. There are three bedrooms in our ___ .

13. The football game starts in one ___ .

out	found	around	cloud	hour
about	ground	sound	mouth	house
count	round	loud	south	mouse

B Complete each phrase with a spelling word.

1. not **in**, but ____

2. not **lost**, but ____

3. not **north**, but ____

4. not **square**, but ____

5. not the **sky**, but the ____

6. not **quiet**, but ____

7. not a **minute**, but an ____

8. not a **cat**, but a ____

C Print the spelling word that rhymes with the clue and fits in the shape.

1. shout

4. south

2. hound

5. proud

3. mount

6. round

20

Follow the directions to change each clue word into two spelling words.

1. **hound**   Change **h** to **s** to make <u>sound</u>.

              Change **s** to **r** to make ___.

2. **mount**   Change **nt** to **th** to make ___.

              Change **m** to **s** to make ___.

3. **grouch**   Change **ch** to **nd** to make ___.

              Change **g** to **a** to make ___.

4. **shout**   Change **sh** to **ab** to make ___.

              Take off **ab** to make ___.

5. **proud**   Change **pr** to **cl** to make ___.

              Take off **c** to make ___.

6. **mound**   Change **nd** to **se** to make ___.

              Change **m** to **h** to make ___.

Reach Out for New Words

A Find and write the eight new **ou** words in this puzzle.

B Write the new **ou** word that matches each meaning.

1. shirt

2. sofa

3. not indoors

4. how much

5. a powder for baking

6. very high hill

7. stream of water

8. to search for

bed	+ s =	beds	*beds*
leg	+ s =	legs	*legs*
step	+ s =	steps	*steps*
flag	+ s =	flags	*flags*
clock	+ s =	clocks	*clocks*
fox	+ es =	foxes	*foxes*
box	+ es =	boxes	*boxes*
inch	+ es =	inches	*inches*
lunch	+ es =	lunches	*lunches*
dish	+ es =	dishes	*dishes*
wish	+ es =	wishes	*wishes*
brush	+ es =	brushes	*brushes*
bus	+ es =	buses	*buses*
glass	+ es =	glasses	*glasses*
class	+ es =	classes	*classes*

A word that names something is called a **noun**. A noun that names one thing is a **singular** noun. A noun that names more than one thing is a **plural** noun.

1. The nouns in the first column are singular nouns.
   How many end with **x**? with **ch**? with **s**? with **sh**?

2. The nouns in the second column are plural nouns. What one letter has been added to some words? What two letters have been added to other words?

Make many nouns plural by adding **s**.
When a noun ends with **x**, **ch**, **s**, or **sh**, add **es** to make the plural form.

Practice the Words

A Write the spelling words that complete these sentences.

1. Tom will wash the ___ after dinner.

2. My sister packed our ___ in brown bags.

3. Three ___ just left the station.

4. This belt is twenty ___ long.

5. Drink three ___ of milk each day.

6. We walked up the ___ to the next floor.

7. Two ___ were flying from the same pole.

8. My brother and I sleep in bunk ___ .

9. The school ___ were ten minutes fast.

10. The ___ had bushy red tails.

11. Mary packed the books in cardboard ___ .

12. All of the painter's ___ need cleaning.

13. A spider has eight ___ .

14. My sister ___ she had a puppy.

foxes	lunches	brushes	classes	steps
boxes	dishes	buses	beds	flags
inches	wishes	glasses	legs	clocks

B Look at each word. If it is spelled correctly, draw a ☺.
If it is misspelled, write the word correctly.

1. flages
2. glasses
3. foxes
4. steps
5. clases

6. inchs
7. buses
8. clockes
9. brushs
10. wishs

C Unscramble each group of letters to make a singular word. Then
write its plural form. The first word is done for you.

Singular

Plural

1. slags   <u>glass</u>   <u>glasses</u>
2. ofx
3. deb
4. huncl
5. spet
6. sub
7. oxb
8. hids
9. elg
10. scals

25

foxes   lunches   brushes   classes   steps

boxes   dishes   buses   beds   flags

inches   wishes   glasses   legs   clocks

Build Word Power

Unscramble each group of words to make a sentence. The first word has a capital letter. Put a period at the end of each sentence. Circle each spelling word.

1. flags the at Look.   Look at the (flags)

2. up Walk steps the.

3. lunch ate The foxes.

4. bed near The clock my is.

5. box The is tall inches six.

6. dishes Wash and glasses the the.

26

Search for new words!
Follow the directions below.

Reach Out for New Words

A Find the correct path through this maze. Words that add **es** to make the plural form are on the correct path. Write the seven words that are on the correct path.

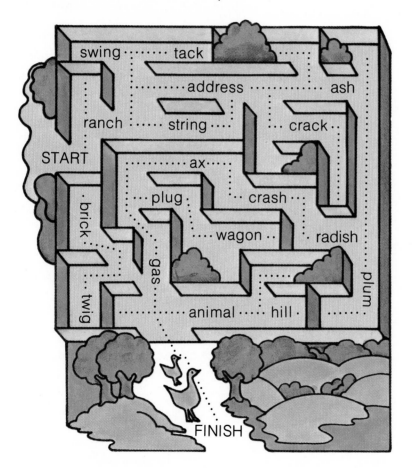

B Write the plural form of each word that was on the correct path through the maze.

toy	toys	*toys*
cowboy	cowboys	*cowboys*
day	days	*days*
bay	bays	*bays*
ray	rays	*rays*
play	plays	*plays*
tray	trays	*trays*
runway	runways	*runways*
bluejay	bluejays	*bluejays*
birthday	birthdays	*birthdays*
key	keys	*keys*
monkey	monkeys	*monkeys*
turkey	turkeys	*turkeys*
donkey	donkeys	*donkeys*
valley	valleys	*valleys*

1. The nouns in the first column end with the letter _____.

2. Is the letter before each final **y** a vowel?

3. The nouns in the second column are plural.

   What letter has been added to form the plural?

When a noun ends with **vowel + y**, add the letter **s** to form the plural.

A Write the spelling words that complete these sentences.

1. The drama club gave two <u>plays</u> this year.

2. Airplanes land on ___.

3. Most ___ know how to ride horses.

4. Two ___ pulled the hay wagon.

5. My aunt raises geese and ___.

6. The map showed rivers, seas, and ___.

7. My mother works three ___ a week.

8. The ___ of the sun give us light.

9. Sue put her games and ___ away.

10. Put all the glasses on those ___.

11. Bob and Rosa's ___ are both in May.

12. Dad lost all the ___ to the house.

13. Low places between hills are called ___ .

B Add the missing vowels to complete each word. Then write the plural form.

1. c__wb__y
2. b__rthd__y
3. m__nk__y
4. t__rk__y
5. r__nw__y
6. v__ll__y

Dictionary

Words in the dictionary are listed in **alphabetical order**.

a b c d e f g h i j k l m n o p q r s t u v w x y z

C Write each group of words in alphabetical order. When two or more words begin with the same letter, look at the second letter.

lamp
like
luck

1	2
donkeys	turkeys
bays	toys
keys	runways
days	trays
bluejays	rays

toys	bays	trays	birthdays	turkeys
cowboys	rays	runways	keys	donkeys
days	plays	bluejays	monkeys	valleys

Build Word Power

Writing

Read these ABC poems.

A yellow ball
bounced over the
car and
dropped in the street.

Kittens
like to
meow and
nap in the sunshine.

Use spelling words to write two of your own ABC poems. The beginning letters of the lines are in alphabetical order. You may start the first line with any letter.

Search for new words!
Follow the directions below.

Reach Out for New Words

A Look at the word in each space. Find and write the eight words
that end in a **vowel + y**.

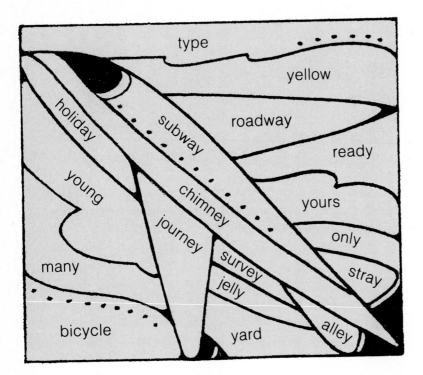

B Write the plural form of each new word.

32

fly	flies	*flies*
city	cities	*cities*
copy	copies	*copies*
baby	babies	*babies*
lady	ladies	*ladies*
pony	ponies	*ponies*
daisy	daisies	*daisies*
party	parties	*parties*
candy	candies	*candies*
cherry	cherries	*cherries*
bunny	bunnies	*bunnies*
puppy	puppies	*puppies*
penny	pennies	*pennies*
berry	berries	*berries*
butterfly	butterflies	*butterflies*

1. Each word in the first column ends with the letter _____.

2. The letters **a**, **e**, **i**, **o**, and **u** are called _____.
   The other letters of the alphabet are called **consonants**.

3. Do the words in the first column have a <u>consonant</u> or a <u>vowel</u> before the final **y**?

4. The nouns in the second column are plural.
   What are the last three letters of these words?

To make the plural form of a noun that ends with **consonant + y**, change the **y** to **i** and add **es**.

33

flies   babies   daisies   cherries   pennies

cities   ladies   parties   bunnies   berries

copies   ponies   candies   puppies   butterflies

Practice the Words

A Use each clue to find a spelling word that fits in the boxes.

1. little children

2. young dogs

3. large towns

4. birthday _____

5. cents

6. small fruits

7. bugs

8. women

9. writes again

10. chocolates

11. baby rabbits

Proofreading

B Find each misspelled word. Write the word correctly.

1. The butterflis landed on the daises.
   (2 words)

2. We ate ice cream with beries at the partie.
   (2 words)

3. The ponis brushed the flys off their backs.
   (2 words)

4. The ladies bought cherrys at the fruit stand.
   (1 word)

Dictionary

C Write each group of words in alphabetical order. When two or more words begin with the same letter, look at the second letter.

1	2
candies	pennies
babies	ponies
copies	ladies
cities	puppies
bunnies	parties
cherries	daisies

flies   babies   daisies   cherries   pennies

cities   ladies   parties   bunnies   berries

copies   ponies   candies   puppies   butterflies

Build Word Power

Follow the directions for changing each clue word into the singular form of a spelling word. Write each word. Then write the plural form of the word.

	Clue	Change	Singular	Plural
1.	buddy	**dd** to **nn**	bunny	bunnies
2.	parts	**s** to **y**	___	___
3.	pity	**p** to **c**	___	___
4.	lazy	**z** to **d**	___	___
5.	pond	**d** to **y**	___	___
6.	peppy	**pp** to **nn**	___	___
7.	belly	**ll** to **rr**	___	___
8.	carry	**rr** to **nd**	___	___
9.	puffy	**ff** to **pp**	___	___
10.	body	**od** to **ab**	___	___
11.	fry	**r** to **l**	___	___
12.	cone	**ne** to **py**	___	___
13.	dairy	**r** to **s**	___	___
14.	merry	**m** to **ch**	___	___

New Words spy body ferry family company
army enemy duty bakery

Reach Out for New Words

A Words are printed in three directions in this puzzle. → ↓ ↘ Find
nine **consonant + y** words. Write each word.

```
b o d y h b c
a f e r r y o
k f a j d g m
e a r m y m p
r s p y i k a
y d u t y l n
c l e n e m y
```

B Write the plural form of each new word.

man	men	*men*
woman	women	*women*
foot	feet	*feet*
tooth	teeth	*teeth*
mouse	mice	*mice*
deer	deer	*deer*
sheep	sheep	*sheep*
elf	elves	*elves*
calf	calves	*calves*
wolf	wolves	*wolves*
shelf	shelves	*shelves*
leaf	leaves	*leaves*
loaf	loaves	*loaves*
wife	wives	*wives*
knife	knives	*knives*

1. How many words change their spelling to make the plural form?
2. How many plural words are the same as the singular words?
3. How many words change **f** or **fe** to **v** and add **es** to make the plural form?

Some nouns make the plural form in an unusual way.
Sometimes a new word is used.
Sometimes the same word is used for both the singular and plural forms.
Some nouns that end with **f** or **fe** change the **f** or **fe** to **v** and add **es** to make the plural form.

38

Practice the Words

A Make three columns on your paper as shown below.
Write the singular words in alphabetical order in the first column.
Then complete the chart.

	Singular Form	Plural Form	How many letters are the same?
1.	calf	calves	3
2.	—	—	—
3.	—	—	—
4.	—	—	—
5.	—	—	—
6.	—	—	—
7.	—	—	—
8.	—	—	—
9.	—	—	—
10.	—	—	—
11.	—	—	—
12.	—	—	—
13.	—	—	—
14.	—	—	—
15.	—	—	—

men   feet   mice   sheep   calves   shelves   loaves   knives
women   teeth   deer   elves   wolves   leaves   wives

B Write the spelling word that fits each clue.

1. what books are kept on

2. things that grow on trees

3. married women

4. used for cutting

5. bread comes in these

6. small people in folk tales

7. baby cows

8. wild animals that howl

C Add the missing letters to make plural words.

1. m _ c _

2. f _ e _

3. w _ m _ n

4. m _ n

5. s _ e _ p

6. d _ e _

7. t _ e _ h

8. w _ l _ e _

40

m	a	e	s	l	h	v	w	z	k	p	d	i
1	2	3	4	5	6	7	8	9	10	11	12	13

g	t	j	o	r	c	f	y	u	q	n	b	x
14	15	16	17	18	19	20	21	22	23	24	25	26

Build Word Power

Each number in this code stands for one letter of the alphabet.
Decode each word and write it.

One Friday evening, Mr. Wilson and his 8 13 20 3

baked thirteen 5 17 2 7 3 4 of their famous bread

to sell at the town fair. They stored the bread on their kitchen

 4 6 3 5 7 3 4 .

Later that night the Wilsons heard 5 3 2 7 3 4

rustling outside their bedroom window. At first they thought

 8 17 5 7 3 4 were after their 4 6 3 3 11 or

 19 2 5 7 3 4 . Then a window opened. Two

 8 17 1 3 24 climbed in, wearing soft slippers on their

 20 3 3 15 . As quietly as 3 5 7 3 4 the Wilsons

followed them toward the kitchen. There they were, eating the

loaves of bread!

New Words   oxen   lives   geese   halves

thieves   children   yourselves

Reach Out for New Words

A Words are printed in three directions in this puzzle. → ↓ ↘ Find the singular form of each new word. Then write it.

```
y  h  f  j  d  n  k  p
g  o  o  s  e  p  l  s
m  x  u  f  q  l  g  q
c  v  g  r  k  i  y  v
c  w  d  t  s  f  h  n
t  h  i  e  f  e  a  r
z  h  b  c  h  i  l  d
b  x  r  j  s  m  f  f
```

Proofreading

B Find each misspelled word. Write the word correctly.

1. The childrun divided the cake into two haves.
(2 words)

2. Two thiefs stole our gooses.
(2 words)

3. These oxes have spent their whole lifes on our farm.
(2 words)

4. Did you build this cabin yourselfs?
(1 word)

1.
place
prize
once

2.
boat
coat
road

3.
out
about
sound

4.
bed   beds
dish   dishes
glass glasses

5.
toy   toys
birthday birthdays
key   keys

6.
city   cities
party parties
penny pennies

7.
woman women
wolf   wolves
knife knives

A Look at the first pair of words in each row. In what way do these words go together? Write a spelling word that makes the second pair of words go together in the same way as the first pair.

1. **boat** is to **boats**   as   **bed** is to $\underline{beds}$

2. **penny** is to **pennies**   as   **party** is to ___

3. **man** is to **men**   as   **woman** is to ___

4. **dishes** is to **dish**   as   **glasses** is to ___

5. **toy** is to **toys**   as   **key** is to ___

6. **pennies** is to **penny**   as   **cities** is to ___

7. **wolves** is to **wolf**   as   **knives** is to ___

8. **key** is to **keys**   as   **birthday** is to ___

Proofreading

B Find each misspelled word. Write the word correctly.

1. I onse saw some wolfes in the woods.
   (2 words)

2. There is no plase to stop along this rode.
   (2 words)

3. The boat docked at two citys in Maine.

(1 word)

4. One of the women won the prise.

(1 word)

5. Get the glasas and dishs for the party.

(2 words)

6. My keys fell aut of my pocket.

(1 word)

C Find the word from the box that goes in each blank.
Write each word.

knives	pennies	out	sound
coat	about	toys	boat

1. sharp ____

2. cost ten ____

3. ____ of time

4. read ____ dogs

5. row the ____

6. a winter ____

7. play with ____

8. a loud ____

A Write the fifteen words on your paper.
Then follow these directions.

1. Put a ✔ in front of each word that ends in **x**, **ch**, **sh**.
Write the plural of these words.

2. Underline each **vowel + y** word.
Write the plural of these words.

3. Put a ⬭ around each **consonant + y** word.
Write the plural of these words.

4. There should be four words left that have not been marked.
Write the plural for each one.

✔ 1. brush   <u>brushes</u>

2. baby

3. box

4. goat

5. donkey

6. puppy

7. deer

8. bay

9. flag

10. tray

11. pony

12. lady

13. foot

14. inch

15. day

B Three words in each row follow the same spelling pattern. One word does not. Find that word. Be ready to tell why it does not belong.

1. step   mile   lake   race

    (Only the word **step** does not end with a silent **e**.)

2. south   float   toast   oak

3. feet   teeth   sheep   flies

4. count   since   around   ground

5. toads   lunches   clocks   clouds

6. cowboys   plays   candies   turkeys

7. puppy   runway   bunny   berry

C Look at the first pair of words in each row. In what way do these words go together? Write a word from the box to make the second pair of words go together in the same way as the first pair.

round   calves   candies   mouth   monkeys

1. **bones** are to **dogs**   as   **bananas** are to <u>monkeys</u>

    (Dogs like bones.)   (Monkeys like bananas.)

2. **dog** is to **puppies**   as   **cow** is to____

3. **sour** is to **lemons**   as   **sweet** is to ____

4. **smell** is to **nose**   as   **taste** is to ____

5. **box** is to **square**   as   **ball** is to ____

47

picnic	pile	hamburger	creek
poured	logs	lemonade	awful
grapes	ants	sparrow	bananas
burned	fire	blanket	napkins

Prewriting. Prewriting means getting ready to write. You must think about what you want to say before you begin writing.

Use Prewriting Skills

Use the spelling words to plan a story about a picnic in the woods.

1. What four things will you have to eat and drink?

2. You will need a fire to cook the food. What two words go with the word **fire**?

3. What are two other things that you will bring for the picnic?

4. What three animals or other things might you see in the woods?

Now Think   What kind of picnic will you write about? Will it be a wonderful picnic or an awful picnic? Write your story idea on your own paper.

Writing. Stories often begin with a sentence that tells the main idea or the most important thing about the story. That sentence is called a **topic sentence.**

Use Writing Skills

A On your own paper, write two good topic sentences for a story about a picnic. Begin your sentences with the word groups below.

1. Picnics can be ____ .

2. On our picnic last week, ____ .

A sentence must be a complete thought. Sometimes a group of words is not a sentence. You must add words to make the thought complete.

Incomplete thought: *Logs for the fire*

Complete sentence: We need more *logs for the fire.*
The *logs for the fire* are too wet to burn.

B Look at the groups of words below. Add words to make each group into a complete sentence. Write the sentences on your own paper.

1. burned the hamburgers

4. deer crossing the creek

2. a pile of ants

5. poured the lemonade

3. bananas and grapes

6. spilled on the blanket

Now Write

The first time you write your story is like a practice. It is called a **first draft,** or a rough draft. Write a first draft of your story. Follow the directions.

1. Begin with a topic sentence. Do you want to use one of the topic sentences you wrote for Exercise A?

2. Read the sentences you wrote for Exercise B. Will some fit your story?

Revising and Proofreading. Revising means changing parts of your story to make it better. Follow two steps to revise your writing.

1. Read your story aloud. Change any of the ideas or sentences you want to make better.
2. Proofread your writing. Look at your writing carefully to find mistakes in capitalization, punctuation, and spelling.

Use Revising and Proofreading Skills

A Practice revising the ideas in the story below.

1. Find the two groups of words that are incomplete thoughts.
2. Make the two groups of words into complete sentences by adding words.

My birthday picnic started out to be fun. Mom parked the car on a dirt road. Near the lake. First we found a good place to eat lunch. Then we put a blanket on the ground. The food, the napkins, and the dishes, too. Just as we were about to eat, we heard a loud sound. It was thunder. Suddenly, the sun was gone and one big cloud came over our picnic. Everything was soaking wet before we could count to ten. The end of my party was not much fun.

B Practice your proofreading skills. Find the mistakes and rewrite the story correctly.

1. Find the six misspelled words. Write the words correctly.
2. Find and correct two capitalization errors.
3. Find and correct three punctuation mistakes.

Some mistakes are already marked.

Remember
- A sentence begins with a capital letter and ends with a period.
- A question ends with a question mark.
- A speaker's words begin and end with quotation marks.

Sue and I went for a walk in the woods to pick berries. After a while we found some berry bushes and began to fill our boxs. Soon We heard a sound in a pile of leafs Sue asked, "What was that." I said, "It was just a fat old tode jumping off a stone. Then we heard another sound This time it was two baby bunnies they were chasing butterflys. we stopped onse more on the way home to watch some sparrows. then we went to my house to tell everyone about the fat old toad and the silly bunnys.

Now Revise   Read the first draft of your story. Be sure your sentences are complete. Proofread and correct any punctuation and spelling mistakes. Write your final copy in your best handwriting.

A Writer's Journal

UNIT TWO

You can get ideas for writing in your journal by looking at things around you. Some things—like a big red balloon or a yellow sunflower—are easy to notice. But have you ever stopped and really looked at a leaf or the bark of a tree?

Looking at things carefully can help you become a better writer. In the paragraph below, the writer tells how to look at something as simple as a leaf.

Read the paragraph. Try to picture in your mind the things the writer describes. Then discuss the questions with the class.

Look at it as though you had never seen a withered green-and-yellow leaf before in your whole life. What does it make you think of? Start with its colors. Green and yellow. Reach back into *your* private store of remembered things for pictures that match the yellow and green on the leaf. You've seen lots of yellow things, and lots of green things, and lots of yellow-and-green things. Get your notebook and write down every single one you can think of:

yellow butter and yellow butterflies and
yellow mittens and yellow beads and
yellow fish and yellow lemon drops and
yellow paper towels and a yellow sun.

Green soda bottle and green frogs and
green seesaws and green cat eyes and green giants.

Green-and-yellow tie-dyed shirts and
green-and-yellow pinwheels and
green-and-yellow turtle bellies and
green-and-yellow snakes and
green-and-yellow Play-Doh that got mixed together
by mistake.

—SYLVIA CASSEDY
from *In Your Own Words*

Talking About the Paragraph

1. What does the green-and-yellow leaf make *you* think of? What other things have *you* seen that are yellow, or green, or yellow and green?

2. What is meant by "*your* private store of remembered things"?

3. Why does the author tell you to write things in a notebook? How might the notes help you later in your other writing?

Writing in Your Journal

Maybe the paragraph has given you an idea for your next journal entry. If you need help getting started, use one of these:

1. Look around you. Choose something you see to write about. Tell what it is and what its color makes you think of.

2. Pick a color. Reach back into your memory for pictures of things that match that color. List the things you think of. For example: Orange is carrots, a jack-o-lantern, and a bright sunset.

Building a Personal Word List

When you are writing, you may want to use a word you do not know how to spell. If this happens, follow these steps:

1. Write the word as you think it should be spelled.

2. After you have finished writing, check to see if the word is on your personal word list. If not, look up the word in the dictionary.

3. Correct your spelling and add the word to your personal word list.

4. Practice spelling the word several times.

pass	*pass*
dress	*dress*
guess	*guess*
toss	*toss*
across	*across*
press	*press*
unless	*unless*
all	*all*
pull	*pull*
full	*full*
roll	*roll*
spell	*spell*
shell	*shell*
still	*still*
shall	*shall*

1. How many words end with the letters **ll**?
2. How many words end with the letters **ss**?

Many words end with double consonants.

Practice the Words

A Find pairs of spelling words that rhyme with each other and fit in the shapes. Write the words.

1.

2.

3.

4.

Proofreading

B Find each misspelled word. Write the word correctly.

1. Which dres shal I wear?
(2 words)

2. Please pass the salt accros the table.
(1 word)

3. I stil have all the money Dad gave me.
(1 word)

4. Don't pres the button unnless you want to change your answer.
(2 words)

55

Dictionary

The two words at the top of each page in the dictionary are called **guide words.** The guide word on the left tells you the first word on the page. The guide word on the right tells you the last word on the page. All the words on the page are listed in alphabetical order between the two guide words.

guide word   guide word

tall   **vest**

tall ═══════════

vest ═══════════

C   The word pairs below are guide words. What spelling words go on each page? Write them in alphabetical order.

pass	pull
dress	full
guess	roll
toss	spell
across	shell
press	still
unless	shall
all	

1. **about/duck**
   (3 words)

2. **fall/home**
   (2 words)

3. **park/roof**
   (4 words)

4. **shake/until**
   (6 words)

Writing

Write riddles for three of your spelling words. Ask a friend to guess the answers.

Use two clues in each riddle. The first clue should tell the meaning of the word. The second clue can give the number of letters, a rhyming word, or some other hint. Write your answer.

Clues

It means not empty.

It sounds like pull.

full

Reach Out for New Words

A Find the letters that fit in the blanks to make new words. Write
each word.

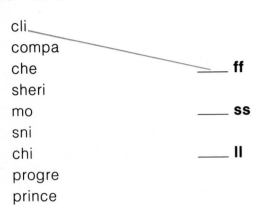

cli

compa

che ———— **ff**

sheri

mo ———— **ss**

sni

chi ———— **ll**

progre

prince

cliff

B Use each clue to find one of the new words that fits in the boxes.
Write each word.

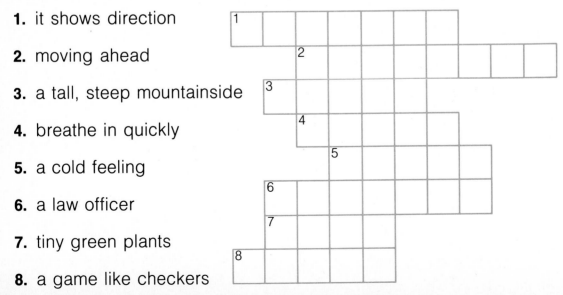

1. it shows direction

2. moving ahead

3. a tall, steep mountainside

4. breathe in quickly

5. a cold feeling

6. a law officer

7. tiny green plants

8. a game like checkers

Words with double consonants in the middle

dollar	*dollar*
follow	*follow*
gallon	*gallon*
swallow	*swallow*
butter	*butter*
cotton	*cotton*
pretty	*pretty*
tomorrow	*tomorrow*
sorry	*sorry*
pepper	*pepper*
happen	*happen*
ribbon	*ribbon*
lesson	*lesson*
ladder	*ladder*
dinner	*dinner*

1. How many words have the letters **ll**?
2. How many words have the letters **tt**?
3. What other double letters do you see?

Many words are spelled with double consonants in the middle.

59

dollar	swallow	pretty	pepper	lesson
follow	butter	tomorrow	happen	ladder
gallon	cotton	sorry	ribbon	dinner

A Use each clue to find a spelling word that fits in the puzzle. Write each word.

Across
2. a meal
4. used like salt
7. something to study
9. a kind of cloth
11. feeling sad
12. something to climb
13. the next day

Down
1. to take place
3. used for bows
5. spread this on bread
6. how milk is measured
8. you do this when you eat
10. beautiful

B Answer each question with spelling words.

1. Which three words have the letters **tt**?

2. Which four words have the letters **ll**?

Dictionary

The words listed on a dictionary page are called **entry words**. They are printed in dark letters to help you find them.

Each entry word is divided into word parts called **syllables**. A dot or space shows where a word is divided into syllables.

---

but·ter (but′ ər) *noun* a spread for bread or cooking made by churning cream.

How many syllables are in the word **butter**?

C Look up each word in your spelling dictionary. Divide it into syllables. Put a dot between the syllables.

1. pretty pret•ty   **8.** ladder

2. sorry   **9.** lesson

3. dinner   **10.** follow

4. dollar   **11.** cotton

5. swallow   **12.** pepper

6. ribbon   **13.** gallon

7. happen   **14.** tomorrow

Writing

Write a sentence with each group of spelling words. Circle the spelling words in each sentence. Remember to start with a capital letter and end with a period.

1. dollar, ribbon, pretty

I paid one (dollar) for this (pretty) yellow (ribbon.)

2. happen, follow, ladder

3. dinner, pepper, butter

4. sorry, gallon, swallow

Reach Out for New Words

A Unscramble the letters and write the new words. Look for the double consonants.

1. nistne

2. abmelulr

3. catit

4. rowra

5. csissros

6. nimlilo

7. nedysdul

8. arctor

B Complete each phrase with one of the new words.

1. not a **bow**, but an ___

2. not a **knife**, but ___

3. not **slowly**, but ___

4. not a **bean**, but a ___

5. not a **basement**, but an ___

6. not a **hundred**, but a ___

7. not **golf**, but ___

8. not a **raincoat**, but an ___

ask	+ ed	=	asked	*asked*
talk	+ ed	=	talked	*talked*
walk	+ ed	=	walked	*walked*
shout	+ ed	=	shouted	*shouted*
plant	+ ed	=	planted	*planted*
close	+ ed	=	closed	*closed*
live	+ ed	=	lived	*lived*
use	+ ed	=	used	*used*
smile	+ ed	=	smiled	*smiled*
tease	+ ed	=	teased	*teased*
save	+ ed	=	saved	*saved*
chase	+ ed	=	chased	*chased*
hike	+ ed	=	hiked	*hiked*
tie	+ ed	=	tied	*tied*
wade	+ ed	=	waded	*waded*

A **verb** is a word that tells about an action.
A verb that tells about an action that happened in the past is in the **past tense**.

1. The words in the first column can all tell about an action. They are called ____.
2. What two letters were added in the last column to put the verbs in the past tense?
3. How many words in the first column end with **silent e**?
   What happened to the final **e** before **ed** was added?

Make the past tense of many verbs by adding **ed**.
When a verb ends in **silent e**, drop the **e** before you add **ed**.

A Write the spelling words that complete these sentences.

1. Alice ___ the door softly.

2. The monkeys ___ each other.

3. The painter ___ a large brush.

4. My family once ___ in Canada.

5. Tina ___ the kitten's life.

6. The teacher ___ a hard question.

7. Carl ___ to school today.

8. The dog ___ the cat up a tree.

9. The fans ___ with excitement.

10. Dad ___ on the telephone for an hour.

11. The happy child ___ at the clown.

12. We ___ a small tree in our yard.

13. Bobby ___ a bow on the present.

14. The children ___ in the shallow water.

The **base form** of a word is the word before any changes have been made.

The base form of **shouted** is **shout**.

B Read each sentence. Then follow the directions below each sentence.

1. Do you live in this building?
(Write the base form of **lived**.)

2. Carl ___ tulips in the garden.
(Write the past tense of **plant**.)

3. We always ___ when our team wins.
(Write the base form of **shouted**.)

4. I ___ past that store every day.
(Write the base form of **walked**.)

5. Ron ___ Lois to help him.
(Write the past tense of **ask**.)

6. The farmer will ___ a strong hoe.
(Write the base form of **used**.)

7. The owners ___ the store at night.
(Write the base form of **closed**.)

8. My sister ___ her money.
(Write the past tense of **save**.)

9. The scouts ___ through the forest.
(Write the past tense of **hike**.)

10. Do all dogs ___ cars?
(Write the base form of **chased**.)

asked	shouted	lived	teased	hiked
talked	planted	used	saved	tied
walked	closed	smiled	chased	waded

C Unscramble each group of letters to make a word. Write each word. Then add **ed** to each word to make it a spelling word.

1. klaw

2. touhs

3. vile

4. secol

5. kalt

6. seate

7. miles

8. keih

9. iet

10. dewa

Build Word Power

Each word below is part of a spelling word. Write the spelling word.

1. mile   <u>smiled</u>

2. us

3. ant

4. lose

5. ease

6. has

7. out

8. as

67

Search for new words!
Follow the directions below.

Reach Out for New Words

A In this puzzle, each number is written twice. Find the silent **e**
word in each pair of numbers. Write the word.

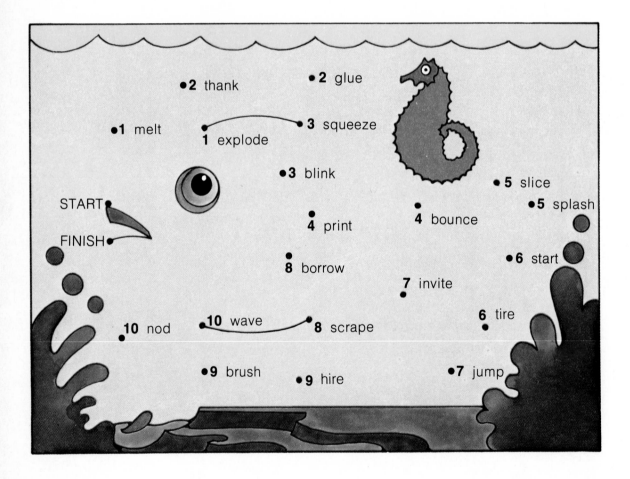

•2 thank

•2 glue

•1 melt

3 squeeze

1 explode

•3 blink

•5 slice

START

•5 splash

FINISH

4 print

4 bounce

8 borrow

•6 start

7 invite

6 tire

10 nod

10 wave

8 scrape

•9 brush

•9 hire

•7 jump

B Write the past tense of each new silent **e** word.

play	+ ed =	played	*played*	
stay	+ ed =	stayed	*stayed*	
spray	+ ed =	sprayed	*sprayed*	
sway	+ ed =	swayed	*swayed*	
obey	+ ed =	obeyed	*obeyed*	
enjoy	+ ed =	enjoyed	*enjoyed*	
cry	+ ed =	cried	*cried*	
fry	+ ed =	fried	*fried*	
dry	+ ed =	dried	*dried*	
try	+ ed =	tried	*tried*	
pry	+ ed =	pried	*pried*	
carry	+ ed =	carried	*carried*	
hurry	+ ed =	hurried	*hurried*	
study	+ ed =	studied	*studied*	
worry	+ ed =	worried	*worried*	

1. The words in the first column can all be action words or ____.
2. How many words in the first column end with **vowel + y**?
   Is the base word changed before **ed** is added?
3. How many verbs in the first column end with **consonant + y**?
   Change the ____ to ____ before you add **ed**.
4. The verbs in the last column are in the ____ tense.

When a verb ends with **vowel + y**, add the ending **ed** to make the past tense.
When a verb ends with **consonant + y**, change the **y** to **i** before you add **ed**.

69

played	swayed	cried	tried	hurried
stayed	obeyed	fried	pried	studied
sprayed	enjoyed	dried	carried	worried

Practice the Words

A Write the spelling words that complete these sentences.

1. The sun ___ up the puddles.

2. Linda was late so she ___ to school.

3. I ___ eating the ___ chicken.

4. The children ___ indoors and ___ games.

5. The pirates ___ open the treasure chest.

6. We ___ the bags to the car.

7. My baby brother ___ all night.

8. Jane ___ not to laugh.

9. Tom ___ for the math test.

10. The trees ___ back and forth in the wind.

B Add the missing letters to complete these spelling words. Then write the base words.

1. c _ i _ d

2. o _ e _ e _

3. s _ r _ y _ d

4. w _ r _ i _ d

C Write the past tense of each base word that fits in the puzzle.

Across	Down
2. stay	**1.** carry
4. hurry	**2.** study
6. spray	**3.** play
8. worry	**5.** enjoy
11. fry	**7.** sway
12. dry	**9.** pry
13. obey	**10.** try

played	swayed	cried	tried	hurried
stayed	obeyed	fried	pried	studied
sprayed	enjoyed	dried	carried	worried

Build Word Power

Writing

Make up an answer for each question. Use the past tense of the underlined word when you write your sentence.

1. What games did the children p<u>lay</u>?

2. What did your class <u>study</u> this morning?

3. How many of those boxes did you <u>carry</u> upstairs?

4. Where did Luis <u>stay</u> when his parents were away?

5. What did you <u>enjoy</u> most about the circus?

Reach Out for New Words

A Make two columns on your paper.
Write each new word in the correct column.

vowel + y words
(4 words)

consonant + y words
(6 words)

Dictionary

B Look up each word in your spelling dictionary. Divide it into
syllables. Put a dot between the syllables. Then write the past
tense.

1. reply   re·ply   replied

2. marry

3. delay

4. destroy

5. spy

6. multiply

7. deny

8. decay

9. bury

10. employ

lay	laid	*lay*	*laid*
say	said	*say*	*said*
see	saw	*see*	*saw*
fly	flew	*fly*	*flew*
take	took	*take*	*took*
write	wrote	*write*	*wrote*
wake	woke	*wake*	*woke*
win	won	*win*	*won*
ride	rode	*ride*	*rode*
fall	fell	*fall*	*fell*
hold	held	*hold*	*held*
swim	swam	*swim*	*swam*
send	sent	*send*	*sent*
build	built	*build*	*built*
go	went	*go*	*went*

1. The words in the first column can all be action words or ___.
2. The verbs in the second column are in the ___ tense.
3. Do the verbs in the second column have the ending **ed**?

Some verbs do not add the ending **ed** to make the past tense.
A new word is used.

A Make three columns on your paper as shown below.
Write these words in alphabetical order in the first column.
Then complete the chart.

wake   see   say   go   fall

write   win   build   fly   swim

hold   lay   ride   take   send

	Word	Past Tense	How many letters are the same?
1.	build	built	4
2.	___	___	___
3.	___	___	___
4.	___	___	___
5.	___	___	___
6.	___	___	___
7.	___	___	___
8.	___	___	___
9.	___	___	___
10.	___	___	___
11.	___	___	___
12.	___	___	___
13.	___	___	___
14.	___	___	___
15.	___	___	___

A **synonym** is a word that means almost the same as another word.
An **antonym** is a word that means the opposite of another word.

B Complete each sentence with a spelling word.

1. A synonym for **looked** is ____ .

2. An antonym for **lost** is ____ .

3. An antonym for **slept** is ____ .

4. A synonym for **tripped** is ____ .

5. An antonym for **gave** is ____ .

6. A synonym for **talked** is ____ .

7. A synonym for **left** is ____ .

8. An antonym for **dropped** is ____ .

Proofreading

C Find each misspelled word. Write the word correctly.

1. The robin flue to its nest and layed an egg.
   (2 words)

2. Last summer I suam and road my bike.
   (2 words)

3. Bob cent me a story he rote.
   (2 words)

4. Val fell out of the tree house she biult.
   (1 words)

laid	flew	woke	fell	sent
said	took	won	held	built
saw	wrote	rode	swam	went

Build Word Power

Writing

Write a sentence to answer each question. Use the past tense of the underlined word in your sentence.

1. What time did you <u>wake</u> up this morning?

2. What did you <u>write</u> your story about?

3. Which animals did you <u>see</u> at the zoo?

4. Where did you <u>ride</u> your bike?

5. Where did you <u>go</u> this summer?

Reach Out for New Words

A The new words are the past tense forms of the verbs below. Write
the verbs on your paper. Then find each new past tense word in
the puzzle. Then write each word you find next to the correct verb.
The words are printed in three directions in the puzzle. → ↓ ↘

1. feed

2. sweep

3. tear

4. wear

5. spend

6. dig

7. steal

8. understand

u	x	w	h	g	b	f	z	g	f
q	n	v	s	t	m	d	d	g	c
f	e	d	p	b	j	u	p	k	p
x	w	z	e	m	q	g	n	h	l
k	l	v	n	r	b	f	x	z	d
h	c	i	t	s	s	j	b	a
w	w	s	w	e	p	t	d	m	c
r	p	q	s	o	v	o	o	n	l
y	f	d	t	r	r	l	t	o	s
o	k	n	t	o	r	e	j	r	d

B Write the past tense of each verb. Then tell how you changed the
verb to its past tense.

1. wear ___wore___ Change _ear_ to _ore_

2. steal   Change ___ to ___

3. dig   Change ___ to ___

4. tear   Change ___ to ___

5. feed   Drop one ___

6. sweep   Change ___ to ___

7. spend   Change ___ to ___

8. understand   Change ___ to ___

The word ending ing

keep	+ ing =	keeping	*keeping*
find	+ ing =	finding	*finding*
clean	+ ing =	cleaning	*cleaning*
spend	+ ing =	spending	*spending*
buy	+ ing =	buying	*buying*
say	+ ing =	saying	*saying*
hurry	+ ing =	hurrying	*hurrying*
trace	+ ing =	tracing	*tracing*
freeze	+ ing =	freezing	*freezing*
bore	+ ing =	boring	*boring*
drive	+ ing =	driving	*driving*
move	+ ing =	moving	*moving*
rise	+ ing =	rising	*rising*
have	+ ing =	having	*having*
come	+ ing =	coming	*coming*

1. What ending was added to the verbs in the first column to make the verbs in the last column?
2. How many verbs in the first column end with **silent e**?
3. Look at the **silent e** words. What letter was dropped before **ing** was added?

> The ending **ing** can be added to many words.
> When a verb ends with **silent e**, drop the **e** before you add **ing**.

A Write the spelling words that complete these sentences.

1. Ted is ___ his messy room.

2. Mom likes ___ our new car.

3. Allen slept through the ___ movie.

4. Mario is ___ popcorn for the movie.

5. The sun is ___ in the east.

6. Jane is ___ the outline of the map.

7. Kim has been ___ her money on candy.

8. JoAnne is ___ to the game with us.

9. The firefighters were ___ to the fire.

10. Lyle's family is ___ to another town.

11. My toes are ___ from the cold.

12. The hen is ___ her eggs warm.

13. Can you hear what Mrs. Wilson is ___ ?

keeping	spending	hurrying	boring	rising
finding	buying	tracing	driving	having
cleaning	saying	freezing	moving	coming

B Find the misspelled word in each group. Write the word correctly.

1. haveing

writing

buying

carrying

2. liking

keeping

fineding

dancing

3. driving

spending

moving

traceing

Dictionary

Each dictionary entry is made up of an entry word and all the information that follows it.

Many entry words are base words. Words with endings, or **word forms**, are often included in the base word entry.

find (fīnd) *verb* to get back something that has been lost [We *found* the missing book.]
—**found, find′ ing**

For example, the word form **finding** is included in the entry for **find.**

C Write the entry word you would look up to find each word.

1. finding

2. buying

3. driving

4. moving

5. keeping

6. saying

7. rising

8. cleaning

9. spending

10. hurrying

11. having

12. freezing

13. boring

14. coming

keeping spending hurrying boring rising
finding buying tracing driving having
cleaning saying freezing moving coming

Build Word Power

Find the spelling word that means the opposite of each word or phrase. Write the word. Then write its base form.

	Spelling Word	Base Form
1. going	coming	come
2. making a mess		
3. moving slowly		
4. giving away		
5. saving		
6. losing		
7. boiling		
8. standing still		
9. interesting		
10. sinking		

Reach Out for New Words

A Unscramble each group of letters to make the **ing** form of one of the new words. Write the **ing** words.

1. grashin

2. chigntwa

3. nasipirg

4. gleaniv

5. ragginu

6. higgannc

7. snurgircy

8. notrbhige

B Write the **ing** form of each new word that matches each meaning.

1. saying good things

2. going away

3. looking at

4. making different

5. giving some to others

6. running quickly

7. quarreling

8. pestering

83

pin	pinned	*pinned*	pinning	*pinning*
wag	wagged	*wagged*	wagging	*wagging*
beg	begged	*begged*	begging	*begging*
stop	stopped	*stopped*	stopping	*stopping*
skip	skipped	*skipped*	skipping	*skipping*
plan	planned	*planned*	planning	*planning*
tag	tagged	*tagged*	tagging	*tagging*
tip	tipped	*tipped*	tipping	*tipping*

1. Look at the words in the first column.
   How many syllables does each word have?
   How many vowels does each word have?
   How many consonants are at the end of each word?
2. When the endings **ed** and **ing** are added to each word, what happens to the final consonant?

Words that have **1 syllable**   pin
              and **1 vowel**   pin
   and end with **1 consonant**   pin
   follow what is called the **1 + 1 + 1 spelling pattern**.
   Double the final consonant before you add **ed** or **ing**.

Practice the Words

A Print the spelling word that fits in the shapes and rhymes with the clue word.

1. dragging

2. ripping

3. dripped

4. winning

5. bragged

6. mopped

7. pegged

8. fanned

9. hopping

10. sagged

11. grinned

12. fanning

pinned   pinning   skipped   skipping
wagged   wagging   planned   planning
begged   begging   tagged   tagging
stopped   stopping   tipped   tipping

B Unscramble each group of letters to make the base form of a
spelling word. Write the base form. Then write the **ing** form.

1. kips   4. agt   7. awg

2. geb   5. pots   8. itp

3. nalp   6. nip

Dictionary

C Write the dictionary entry word you would look up to find each word
below.

1. pinned   4. skipped   7. wagged

2. tagging   5. begging   8. stopped

3. tipped   6. planned

Writing

Sometimes two sentences tell about ideas that are alike. The sentences may even use some of the same words.

Debbie is planning a party. She is planning a party for Val.

You can put these two sentences together to make one sentence. The underlined words in the second sentence are not needed in the new sentence.

Debbie is planning a party for Val.

Make one sentence from each pair of sentences. The words you do not need in the new sentence are underlined.

1. The bus stopped. It stopped at the corner.

2. Sue is skipping rope. She is skipping as fast as she can.

3. The dog is wagging his tail. He is wagging it because he is happy.

Search for new words!
Follow the directions below.

Reach Out for New Words

A Find the right path through this maze. The words on the correct path follow the **1 + 1 + 1 pattern**. Write the **ed** form of each word.

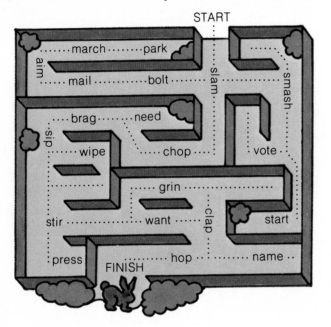

START

march······park

aim

······mail············bolt········

slam

········smash

····brag·······need

sip

·····wipe ······chop····

vote

·······grin············

stir ··············want······

clap

start

press   hop··   ······name··

FINISH

B Use each clue to think of the **ing** form of a word you found in the maze. Each word should fit in the puzzle. Write the words.

1. closing loudly
2. jumping
3. cutting
4. hitting hands
5. drinking
6. mixing
7. smiling
8. boasting

10.
guess
dress
spell

11.
dollar
sorry
pretty

12.
talk   talked
walk   walked
save   saved

13.
play   played
try   tried
study studied

14.
say   said
ride rode
fall fell

15.
buy   buying
hurry hurrying
move   moving

16.
tip   tipped   tipping
stop   stopped stopping
plan   planned planning

A Look at the first pair of words in each row. In what way do these
words go together? Write a spelling word that makes the second
pair of words go together in the same way as the first pair.

1. **study** is to **studied** as **try** is to ___

2. **play** is to **playing** as **buy** is to ___

3. **plan** is to **planning** as **stop** is to ___

4. **study** is to **studying** as **hurry** is to ___

5. **say** is to **said** as **ride** is to ___

6. **rode** is to **ride** as **fell** is to ___

7. **save** is to **saving** as **move** is to ___

8. **dropped** is to **drop** as **tipped** is to ___

Proofreading

B Find each misspelled word. Write the word correctly.

1. I tiped over the prety vase of flowers.
(2 words)

2. Larry tried to spel the long word.
(1 word)

3. Ann siad, "I'm planing on wearing this dress."
(2 words)

4. We wawked to the park and plaied baseball.

C Write the word from the box that goes in each blank.

studied	saved	talked	dollar
dress	guess	sorry	fell

1. I ___ on the phone.

2. I ___ my money.

3. We ___ for the test.

4. I'll ___ the answer.

5. He ___ on the ice.

6. I'm very ___ .

7. She wore a ___ .

8. He spent a ___ .

Using More Review Words

A Write the fifteen words on your paper. Then follow these directions.

1. Put a ▭ around each **silent e** word. Write the past tense.
2. Underline each **vowel + y** word. Write the past tense.
3. Put a ⬭ around each **consonant + y** word. Write the past tense.
4. Put a * after each **1 + 1 + 1 word**. Write the past tense.
5. Write the past tense of the three words you have left.

1. ▭close▭ <u>closed</u>   6. ask   11. use

2. spray   7. obey   12. pry

3. clean   8. tip   13. skip

4. plant   9. smile   14. tag

5. stay   10. study   15. carry

B Three words in each row follow the same spelling pattern. One word does not. Find that word. Be ready to tell why it does not belong.

1. across   pass   pull   ~~gallon~~
   (Only **gallon** has the double letter in the middle.)

2. boring   keeping   freezing   driving

3. woke   rode   pinned   wrote

4. obeyed   worried   dried   fried

5. wagging   spending   begging   tipping

6. trace   rise   have   unless

7. closed   asked   teased   lived

C Look at the first pair of words in each row. Then write a word from the box that makes the second pair of words go together in the same way as the first pair.

dinner	shouted	off	full	tomorrow	flew

1. **in** is to **out**   as   **on** is to ____

2. **present** is to **future**   as   **today** is to ____

3. **fish** is to **swam**   as   **bird** is to ____

4. **bottom** is to **top**   as   **empty** is to ____

5. **noon** is to **lunch**   as   **evening** is to ____

6. **quiet** is to **whispered**   as   **loud** is to ____

milk	sting	pail	rooster
pint	stung	wagon	pumpkin
bees	dozen	honey	turnips
colt	hogs	basket	cabbage

Prewriting. Prewriting means getting ready to write. You must think about what you want to say before you begin writing.

Use Prewriting Skills

Use the spelling words to plan a story about a farm.

1. What four animals might be on the farm?

2. What five foods are on the farm?

3. What three things can you use for carrying?

4. What two words go with **bee**?

Now Think
Think about what a person might see and do on a farm. Do you want to tell a story about someone who visits a farm or someone who lives there? What will the farm look like? Write your story ideas on your own paper.

Use Writing Skills

A Copy each topic sentence below. Choose one word from each pair. See how the words change the setting.

1. Mr. Kapp's (dairy, cattle) farm is a (busy, lonely) place to (live, visit) in the middle of (summer, winter).

2. The morning (frost, sunshine) felt (warm, chilly) as we (walked, ran) to the (barn, field) to help Aunt Laura.

Several ideas can be put together in one sentence. Use commas to separate items in a series of three or more things.

When I woke up, I heard a rooster crowing. I heard bees buzzing. I heard dogs barking.

When I woke up, I heard a rooster crowing, bees buzzing, and dogs barking.

B On your paper, practice putting ideas together into one sentence.

1. Sue was carrying a pail of milk. She was carrying a dozen eggs. She was carrying a jar of honey.

   Sue was carrying ____ .

2. We saw two fat hogs in the barnyard. We saw a skinny colt. We saw a red rooster.

   In the barnyard, we saw ____ .

Now Write   Write the first draft of your farm story. Follow these directions.

1. Begin with a topic sentence that tells about the setting.
2. Decide what will happen in your story. How will it begin? How will it end?

Revising. Revising means changing parts of your story to make it better. Follow two steps to revise your writing.

1. Read your story aloud. Change or add anything that would make it sound better.
2. Proofread your story. Look at your writing carefully to find mistakes in capitalization, punctuation, and spelling.

Use Revising and Proofreading Skills

A Revise the ideas in the story below. Then copy the revised story on your own paper.

1. Find a place where a word is missing. Add the missing word.
2. Find an incomplete thought. Add words to make a complete sentence.
3. Find three sentences that would sound better if they were written as one sentence. As you rewrite, remember to add commas.
4. Find the sentence that would be a good beginning sentence. It tells about the setting. When you rewrite the story, put this sentence first.

I tripped over a pail of milk and scared Kevin. He jumped and dropped the basket of eggs. The inside of the old barn looked spooky when the door closed behind us. We stood still and listened. Squeaking noises. We started looking around. The noises were coming the hay wagon.

"Look!" I said. "It's a cat who came in to have her babies."

The mother cat meowed. Six new kittens were lying beside her. She had two black kittens. She had two white kittens. She had two spotted kittens. Kevin laughed and said, "I never knew cats could squeak like mice!"

B Practice your proofreading skills. Find the mistakes and rewrite the story correctly.

1. Find the six misspelled words. Write them correctly.
2. Find and correct four capitalization errors.
3. Find and correct three punctuation mistakes.

Some mistakes are already marked.

Remember
- A sentence begins with a capital letter and ends with a period.
- Common nouns are not capitalized.
- A comma separates a series of three or more things.

Our Class visit to the animal farm was fun. We were able to pet and feed the animals. The F̶arm had dozins of fences, but no cages. Inside the first fence, we petted two coults, We fed them some oats from a pale Then we fed the sheep the hogs and the Goats. One silly goat tried to eat my lunch baskit and my pumkin pie. Finally, we went to the best place of all. it was a dirt track for pony rides. After we rode on the ponies, a few of us rode around the track in a wagen pulled by a Donkey.

Now Revise   Read the first draft of your story. Be sure your sentences are complete. Check that your story has a beginning, a middle, and an end. Proofread and correct mistakes in capitalization, punctuation, and spelling. Write your final copy in your best handwriting.

A Writer's Journal

Ideas for writing in your journal can come from reading. In the poem below, the writer talks about certain smells. How can something written on a piece of paper help you remember how things smell?

Read this poem. See if the words and phrases the writer uses help you remember smells. Then discuss the questions with your class.

> **"THINK OF TREE"**
> Under
> the car smell
>
> over
> the tar smell
>
> a sweet green and far smell
> flows
> down the street.
>
> And it says
> drifting by,
> > "Think of tree.
> > Think of sky.
> > Think of ripe apples
> > and hay, sun-dry."
>
> Then you know—
> not far away
> they are cutting grass
> in the park today.
>
> —LILIAN MOORE

Talking About the Poem

1. Where does the speaker in the poem live? How can you tell?
2. Where might the speaker have smelled trees and ripe apples? Where might he or she have smelled sun-dried hay?
3. What is the "sweet green and far smell"?
4. What are some of your favorite outdoor smells?

Now read this paragraph. It is from the book *In Your Own Words* by Sylvia Cassedy. It talks about how to sharpen your sense of smell.

Talking About the Paragraph

1. You often hear quiet sounds, but what are quiet smells?
2. What are some ways of discovering quiet smells?

Writing in Your Journal

The poem and the paragraph may have given you ideas about things that may have quiet smells and how you can write about them. Here are some ideas you might use if you need them.

1. Choose your favorite smell—something like bread baking, an orange being peeled, popcorn popping, or the air outside after it rains. Write one sentence about that smell so that someone else could smell it.
2. What is a quiet smell you discovered "by accident"? Describe the smell and how you discovered it.

Some objects that surround you all the time have little quiet smells that you hardly know about. Find out what some of them are. Walk around your living room some time when you don't have a cold, and press your nose against a sofa cushion, a wooden table, the back of the television, a lampshade, a shiny magazine, a telephone book, the soil in a flowerpot. Sometimes you discover these smells by accident, when you are crying into a pillow, for instance, or resting your head on your homework notebook.

Building a Personal Word List

Keeping a personal word list can help you become a better speller. First, the list shows you the words you need to learn to spell. Second, it can help you figure out the kinds of spelling mistakes you make.

As you add words to your personal word list, notice the kinds of spelling mistakes you made. Maybe you forgot to change the **y** to **i** when you wrote **fried**. If you know what kinds of spelling mistakes you make, you may be able to keep them from happening.

fork	fork
born	born
corn	corn
horn	horn
north	north
sport	sport
shorts	shorts
storm	storm
story	story
forget	forget
word	word
worm	worm
world	world
worth	worth
worst	worst

1. What two letters do you see in every word?
2. In how many words do the letters **or** sound like the word **or**?
3. In how many words do the letters **or** sound like **er** in the word **her**?

Many words are spelled with the letters **or**.
The letters **or** may have different sounds.

Practice the Words

A Write the spelling words that complete these sentences.

1. Val likes to eat ___ on the cob.

2. I use a ___ to eat my French fries.

3. Soccer is Nancy's favorite ___.

4. Bob read a ___ about a giant.

5. The ___ kept us awake all night.

6. Lee saw a ___ crawling in the dirt.

7. My baby brother was ___ in January.

8. I spelled one ___ wrong on the test.

9. Canada is ___ of the United States.

10. A globe is a round map of the ___.

11. I like to wear ___ in hot weather.

12. My sister plays a ___ in the band.

13. Did you ___ your lunch money again?

14. How much is that diamond ring ___ ?

fork	horn	shorts	forget	world
born	north	storm	word	worth
corn	sport	story	worm	worst

B Look at each word. If it is spelled correctly, draw a 😊. If it is misspelled, write the word correctly.

1. *story*

2. *werm*

3. *spowrt*

4. *world*

5. *werth*

6. *forek*

7. *born*

8. *noreth*

9. *werd*

10. *wurst*

11. *horn*

12. *fourget*

C Use each clue to find a spelling word that fits in the puzzle. Write each word.

1. opposite of **best**

2. a trumpet

3. a yellow vegetable

4. the earth

5. a fairy tale

6. thunder and lightning

Build Word Power

Writing

A **cinquain** is a poem that has five lines.

Line **1**: a noun

Line **2**: two words <u>describing</u> the noun

Line **3**: three words telling <u>actions</u> of the noun

Line **4**: four words giving a <u>thought</u> or <u>feeling</u> about the noun

Line **5**: a word that means the same as the noun

Storm

Wild, windy

Blows, shrieks, howls

Makes me feel afraid

Tornado

Write cinquains using two of your spelling words.

_____

_____

_____

_____

____

_____

_____

_____

____

New Words   tornado   thorn   corner   record
harbor   acorn   forth   order

Reach Out for New Words

A Find the eight new **or** words in this puzzle. Write each word. Some of the words may overlap.

B Write the new **or** word that matches each meaning.

1. a port

2. a sharp needle on a plant

3. a nut

4. where two streets cross

5. a wind storm

6. it plays music

7. to command

8. forward

paper	*paper*
never	*never*
river	*river*
later	*later*
under	*under*
winter	*winter*
summer	*summer*
number	*number*
over	*over*
water	*water*
herd	*herd*
person	*person*
very	*very*
every	*every*
America	*America*

What two letters do you see in every word?

Many words are spelled with the letters **er**.

paper later summer water very

never under number herd every

river winter over person America

Practice the Words

A Use each clue to find a spelling word that fits in the puzzle. Write each word.

Across

6. 8 is a ___

7. a human being

9. each

10. a large stream

13. a cold season

14. not sooner

Down

1. opposite of **under**

2. a hot season

3. what you write on

4. below

5. Today is ___ hot.

8. not ever

11. what's in a lake

12. group of cows

Proofreading

B Find the misspelled word in each phrase below. Write the word correctly.

1. *number your paeper*

2. *hered of elephants*

3. *have nevre seen*

4. *verry cold winter*

5. *evrey person in the room*

6. *later this sumer*

7. *very deep rivir*

8. *undr the bridge*

9. *United States of Amaerica*

10. *a glass of watter*

Dictionary

C All of these words are entry words in a dictionary.
Look up each word and show how it is divided. Put a dot between the syllables.

1. winter

2. over

3. later

4. number

5. paper

6. never

7. person

8. America

paper	later	summer	water	very
never	under	number	herd	every
river	winter	over	person	America

Build Word Power

Writing

Write four silly sentences. Use two or more **er** words in each sentence. Circle those words.

The (river) freezes every (summer.)

Search for new words!

Follow the directions below.

A Look at the word in each space. Find and write the ten words that have the letters **er**.

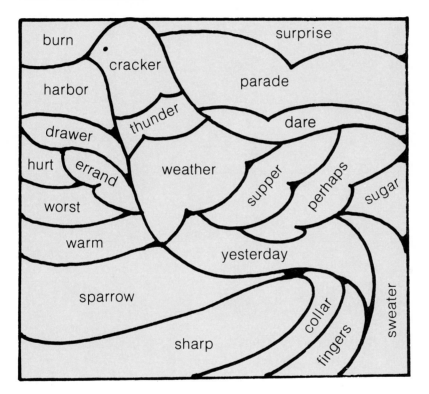

B Unscramble each group of letters to make one of the words you found in the puzzle.

1. styaydeer

2. draner

3. darrew

4. happers

5. reathew

6. kaccerr

7. treeaws

8. trudneh

9. sreppu

10. ringsef

work + er = worker *worker*
lead + er = leader *leader*
paint + er = painter *painter*
pitch + er = pitcher *pitcher*

copy + er = copier *copier*
fly + er = flier *flier*
carry + er = carrier *carrier*

dance + er = dancer *dancer*
bake + er = baker *baker*
skate + er = skater *skater*
wipe + er = wiper *wiper*

win + er = winner *winner*
shop + er = shopper *shopper*
swim + er = swimmer *swimmer*
zip + er = zipper *zipper*

1. The words in the first column are verbs. What two letters have been added to all of the words in the last column?

2. How many verbs in the first column end with **consonant + y**? Change the ___ to ___ before you add **er**.

3. How many verbs end with **silent e**? Drop the ___ before you add **er**.

4. How many verbs follow the **1 + 1 + 1 spelling pattern**? Double the final ___ before you add **er**.

When **er** is added to a verb, the new word tells who or what is doing the action.

A Write the spelling words that complete these sentences.

1. The ___ made rolls and cakes.

2. The sales clerk helped the ___ .

3. Our car needs one new windshield ___ .

4. The ___ fell on the ice.

5. The band ___ raised his arms.

6. The ___ on my jacket is broken.

7. The ___ jumped into the pool.

8. The ___ put on her tap shoes.

9. Tom was the ___ of the race.

10. The airline pilot enjoys being a ___ .

11. The ___ is cleaning her brushes.

12. That beaver is a hard ___ .

13. The ___ struck out three batters in a row.

14. A mail ___ brings the mail to our house.

B Write the spelling word that matches each meaning.

1. someone who flies

2. someone who skates

3. someone who dances

4. someone who leads

5. someone who bakes

6. someone who wins

7. someone who paints

8. someone who swims

9. something that zips

10. something that makes copies

C Find the misspelled word in each group. Write the word correctly.

1. baker
   worker
   carier
   dancer

2. flier
   leader
   swimmer
   wipper

3. picher
   shopper
   painter
   baker

4. zipper
   shoper
   dancer
   leader

5. werker
   skater
   winner
   flier

6. painter
   shopper
   copyer
   swimmer

worker pitcher carrier skater shopper
leader copier dancer wiper swimmer
painter flier baker winner zipper

Build Word Power

Follow the + and − signs to change each clue word into a spelling word. Write the words on your paper.

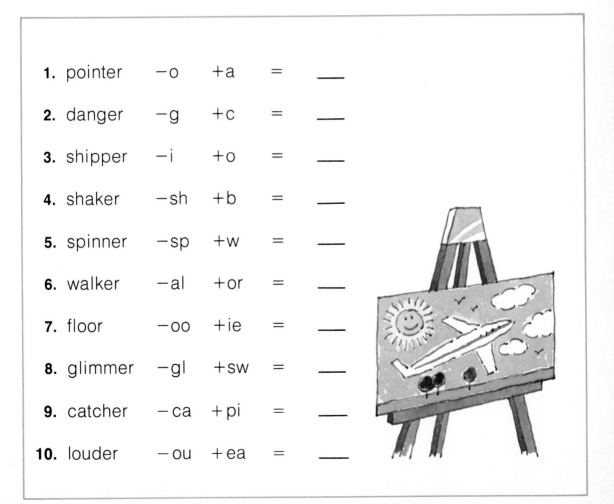

1. pointer −o +a = ___

2. danger −g +c = ___

3. shipper −i +o = ___

4. shaker −sh +b = ___

5. spinner −sp +w = ___

6. walker −al +or = ___

7. floor −oo +ie = ___

8. glimmer −gl +sw = ___

9. catcher −ca +pi = ___

10. louder −ou +ea = ___

New Words speak erase spin supply drum

catch staple drop dip

Reach Out for New Words

A Make four columns on your paper as shown below.
Write each new word in the correct column.

consonant + y	silent e	1 + 1 + 1 word	others
(1 word)	(2 words)	(4 words)	(2 words)

B Words are printed in three different directions in this puzzle.→ ↓ ↘
Find the **er** forms of the nine new words. Then write each word on
your paper.

```
d  i  p  p  e  r  b  b  d  q
r  t  v  d  y  s  x  w  z  c
u  f  r  c  r  l  k  s  p  a
m  j  s  d  q  o  b  u  f  t
m  n  t  p  r  z  p  p  q  c
e  r  a  s  e  r  x  p  w  h
r  w  p  m  p  a  p  l  e  e
g  k  l  h  c  h  k  i  v  r
h  s  e  g  r  j  m  e  t  n
k  j  r  l  m  g  f  r  r  d
s  p  i  n  n  e  r  l  c  n
```

The word ending y

wind	+ y	=	windy	*windy*
sand	+ y	=	sandy	*sandy*
salt	+ y	=	salty	*salty*
luck	+ y	=	lucky	*lucky*
sleep	+ y	=	sleepy	*sleepy*
ice	+ y	=	icy	*icy*
smoke	+ y	=	smoky	*smoky*
shade	+ y	=	shady	*shady*
shine	+ y	=	shiny	*shiny*
grime	+ y	=	grimy	*grimy*
sun	+ y	=	sunny	*sunny*
fog	+ y	=	foggy	*foggy*
fun	+ y	=	funny	*funny*
mud	+ y	=	muddy	*muddy*
bag	+ y	=	baggy	*baggy*

An **adjective** is a word that describes something.

1. What letter was added to all of the nouns in the first column to make the adjectives in the last column?

2. How many nouns in the first column end with **silent e**? Drop the ____ before you add **y**.

3. How many nouns follow the **1 + 1 + 1 spelling pattern**? Double the ____ before you add **y**.

The ending **y** can be added to many nouns.
Nouns with a **y** ending become **adjectives**, or words that describe something.

115

windy   lucky   smoky   grimy   funny

sandy   sleepy   shady   sunny   muddy

salty   icy   shiny   foggy   baggy

Practice the Words

A Use each clue to find a spelling word that fits in the boxes. Write the words.

1. bright and polished

2. has salt

3. misty

4. breezy

5. blocked from the sun

6. covered with mud

7. having good luck

8. slippery

9. hanging loosely

10. covered with dirt and grime

11. tired

12. full of smoke

13. makes you laugh

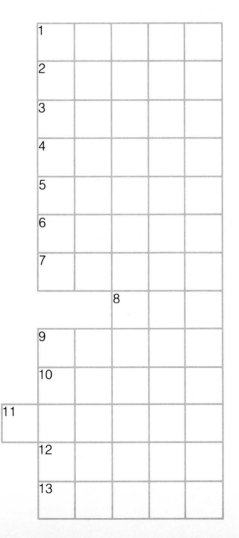

Proofreading

B Find the twelve misspelled words in these sentences. Write each word correctly.

1. The funey clown wore bagy pants and a grimey shirt. He had sleepey eyes and a shinny red nose painted on his face.

2. The morning will be fogy. We are lucky that the afternoon will be warm and suney.

3. Shadey trees grow along the sanddy banks of the mudey river. On a winddy day the water is icey.

Dictionary

Each dictionary entry tells the meaning, or definition, of the entry word.

C Write these words in alphabetical order. Look up each word in your spelling dictionary and complete the definition.

smoky sunny salty lucky sandy

1. ___ = having good ___

2. ___ = tasting of ___

3. ___ = full of ___

4. ___ = filled with ___

5. ___ = bright with ___

windy	lucky	smoky	grimy	funny
sandy	sleepy	shady	sunny	muddy
salty	icy	shiny	foggy	baggy

Build Word Power

Writing

Write new sentences using the **y** form of the underlined word.
Circle the word.

1. The <u>wind</u> is blowing today.

   Today is (windy.)

2. The room is filled with <u>smoke</u>.

3. You have <u>sand</u> on your feet.

4. Your shoes have <u>mud</u> on them.

5. There is <u>ice</u> on the sidewalk.

6. The popcorn has <u>salt</u> on it.

New Words fur squeak grease crunch
noise rain haste star

Reach Out for New Words

A Make three columns on your paper as shown below.
Write each new word in the correct column.

silent e	**1 + 1 + 1**	**other**
(3 words)	(2 words)	(3 words)

m	a	e	s	l	h	v	w	z	k	p	d	i
1	2	3	4	5	6	7	8	9	10	11	12	13

g	t	j	o	r	c	f	y	u	q	n	b	x
14	15	16	17	18	19	20	21	22	23	24	25	26

B Each number in this code stands for one letter of the alphabet.
Decode the missing words in the treasure hunt clues below. Each
word is the **y** form of a new word.

Begin on a _18_ _2_ _13_ _24_ _21_ night . If there is a

_4_ _15_ _2_ _18_ _18_ _21_ sky, you may miss the clue in

your umbrella!

Don't be _6_ _2_ _4_ _15_ _21_ . You might not find the

second clue in the pocket of a _20_ _22_ _18_ _18_ _21_ coat!

Try not to be _24_ _17_ _13_ _4_ _21_ . Look for the clue behind

the _4_ _23_ _22_ _3_ _2_ _10_ _21_ bedroom door!

Don't get your fingers _14_ _18_ _3_ _2_ _4_ _21_ looking!

You will find the last clue under the jar of

_19_ _18_ _22_ _24_ _19_ _6_ _21_ peanut butter!

119

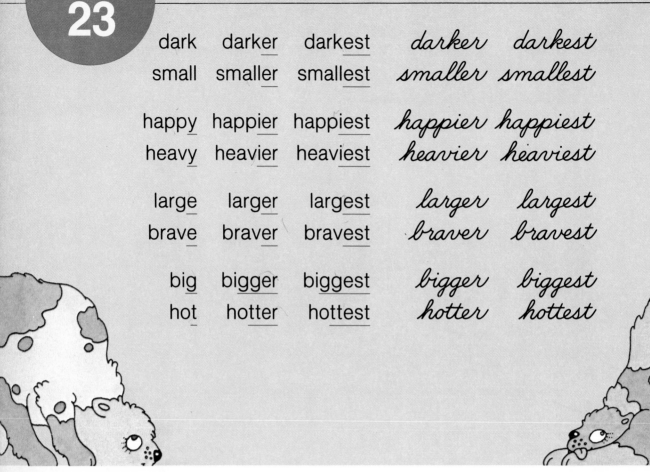

dark	darker	darkest	*darker*	*darkest*
small	smaller	smallest	*smaller*	*smallest*
happy	happier	happiest	*happier*	*happiest*
heavy	heavier	heaviest	*heavier*	*heaviest*
large	larger	largest	*larger*	*largest*
brave	braver	bravest	*braver*	*bravest*
big	bigger	biggest	*bigger*	*biggest*
hot	hotter	hottest	*hotter*	*hottest*

1. The words in the first column are adjectives. What two letters have been added to all of the words in the second column? What three letters have been added in the last column?

2. How many adjectives in the first column end with **consonant + y**? Change the ____ to ____ before you add **er** or **est**.

3. How many adjectives end with **silent e**? Drop the ____ before you add **er** or **est**.

4. How many adjectives follow the **1 + 1 + 1 spelling pattern**? Double the ____ before you add **er** or **est**.

The ending **er** can be added to many adjectives to mean **more**.
The ending **est** can be added to many adjectives to mean **most**.

A Find the missing letters in each word. Then write the word.

1. h_tt_st *hottest*

2. d_rk_r

3. l_r_e_

4. br_v_r

5. h__v__st

6. b_g_e_

7. sm_ll_r

8. l_r_e_t

9. d_r_e_t

10. h_pp__st

11. b_a_e_t

12. s_a__e_t

13. h_t_e_

darker	darkest	braver	bravest
smaller	smallest	bigger	biggest
heavier	heaviest	hotter	hottest
larger	largest	happier	happiest

B Complete each phrase with the **er** or **est** form of the given word. Use **er** to compare two people or things. Use **est** to compare three or more people or things.

1. heavy   ___   of the five boxes

2. dark   ___   hair than yours

3. brave   ___   than Sir Richard

4. big   ___   than my dog

5. large   ___   elephant in the jungle

6. hot   ___   day of the summer

7. big   ___   house in town

8. small   ___   kitten in the litter

9. heavy   ___   than a brick

Dictionary

C The **er** and **est** forms of a word are not listed as entry words in the dictionary. They are often found at the end of the entry for a base word. Write the entry word for each of these adjectives.

1. heavier   **5.** smaller

2. darkest   **6.** bravest

3. hotter   **7.** biggest

4. happiest   **8.** larger

Writing

Write an answer for each question about the clowns. Use the **er** or **est** spelling word that means the same as the underlined words at the left of each sentence.

Grumpy   **Rocko**   **Pinky**

1. <u>most</u> <u>big</u>   Who has the ___ hat?

2. <u>more</u> <u>happy</u>   Which clown is ___ than Rocko?

3. <u>most</u> <u>heavy</u>   Which clown is ___ ?

4. <u>most</u> <u>dark</u>   Who has the ___ hair?

5. <u>more</u> <u>small</u>   Which clown is ___ than Rocko?

New Words	easy	sad	young	lazy	flat
	wet	tame	hungry	wide	

Reach Out for New Words

A Write the **er** form of each new word. Watch out for **silent e**, **consonant + y**, and **1 + 1 + 1** words.

B Write the word that means the opposite of each word or phrase. Use the **est** form of one of the new words.

1. driest
2. most bumpy
3. hardest to do

4. wildest
5. happiest
6. busiest

7. oldest
8. narrowest
9. most full of food

124

wear	*wear*
bear	*bear*
pear	*pear*
tear	*tear*
earn	*earn*
learn	*learn*
earth	*earth*
heard	*heard*
early	*early*
near	*near*
hear	*hear*
year	*year*
fear	*fear*
dear	*dear*
clear	*clear*

1. What three letters do you see in every word?
2. In how many words do the letters **ear** sound like the word **air**?
3. In how many words do the letters **ear** sound like **ur** in the word **turn**?
4. In how many words do the letters **ear** sound like **eer** in the word **deer**?

Many words are spelled with the letters **ear**.
The letters **ear** may have different sounds.

wear	tear	earth	near	fear
bear	earn	heard	hear	dear
pear	learn	early	year	clear

Practice the Words

A Write the spelling words that complete these sentences.

1. Worms live in the ——.

2. I can see through this —— glass.

3. Did you —— that —— growl?

4. Rob wants to —— money for a new bike.

5. Kathy —— an airplane fly over the house.

6. I will get up —— tomorrow morning.

7. Don't —— your good shirt to the picnic.

8. Next —— I will —— how to swim.

9. Did Mike —— his jacket when he fell?

10. My —— friend Kerry is moving —— us.

11. Ben tried to get over his —— of spiders.

Proofreading

B Find each misspelled word. Write the word correctly.

1. *Last yere I learned not to feer the water.*
   (2 words)

2. *Tim herd a bear neer our cabin.*
   (2 words)

3. *Erly this morning the sky was cleer.*
   (2 words)

4. *The roots of the pare tree are deep in the erth.*
   (2 words)

C Write funny answers for these clues. Use two rhyming spelling words for each answer.

1. what 364 days are *near* a *year*

2. a rip made by a
   large furry animal   a ___   ___

3. take a lesson to
   make money   ___ to ___

4. put a fruit on
   your head   ___ a ___

5. listen to someone
   you love   ___ a ___

wear	tear	earth	near	fear
bear	earn	heard	hear	dear
pear	learn	early	year	clear

Build Word Power

Look at the first pair of words in each row. In what way do these words go together? Write a spelling word that makes the second pair of words go together in the same way as the first pair.

1. **puppy** is to **dog**   as   **cub** is to _____

2. **fish** is to **water**   as   **worm** is to _____

3. **eye** is to **see**   as   **ear** is to _____

4. **glass** is to **break**   as   **paper** is to _____

5. **games** are to **play**   as   **lessons** are to _____

6. **flower** is to **rose**   as   **fruit** is to _____

7. **food** is to **tasted**   as   **sound** is to _____

8. **there** is to **here**   as   **far** is to _____

9. **purse** is to **carry**   as   **shirt** is to _____

10. **day** is to **week**   as   **month** is to _____

Search for new words!
Follow the directions below.

Reach Out for New Words

A In this puzzle, each number is written twice. Find and write the **ear** word in each pair of numbers.

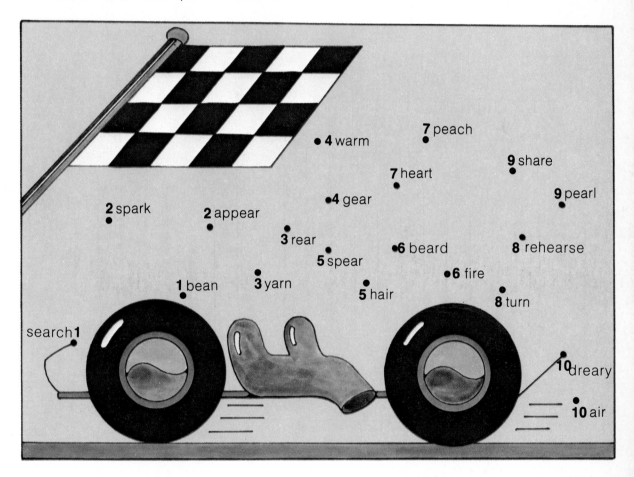

4 warm

7 peach

7 heart

9 share

9 pearl

2 spark

2 appear

4 gear

3 rear

6 beard

8 rehearse

5 spear

6 fire

1 bean

3 yarn

5 hair

8 turn

search 1

10 dreary

10 air

B Unscramble each group of letters to make one of the **ear** words from the puzzle.

1. erra	**3.** plare	**5.** prapea	**7.** yarder	**9.** sheerear
2. drabe	**4.** chears	**6.** thare	**8.** rega	**10.** prase

high	*high*
sigh	*sigh*
thigh	*thigh*
night	*night*
sight	*sight*
fight	*fight*
right	*right*
light	*light*
tight	*tight*
might	*might*
bright	*bright*
flight	*flight*
tonight	*tonight*
frighten	*frighten*
lightning	*lightning*

1. What three letters do you see in every word?

2. Which one of these letters do you hear when you say each word?

3. Which two of these letters are silent?

Many words are spelled with the letters **igh**.
The letters **g** and **h** are silent.

Proofreading

A Write the spelling words that answer each question.

1. Which three words have two syllables?

2. Which three words end with **h**?

3. Which eight words have five letters?

4. Which five words have more than five letters?

B Complete each phrase with a spelling word.

1. a ____ mountain

2. late at ____

3. ____ an enemy

4. an airplane ____

5. with all your ____

6. a ____ of relief

7. ____ shoes

8. thunder and ____

Dictionary

Some words have more than one meaning, or definition, listed in the dictionary. Each definition is given a number.

right (rīt) *adjective* ①correct or true [That is the *right* way to go.] ②opposite of left [Raise your *right* hand.] definition numbers

C Complete each sentence with a word from the box. Look up each word in your spelling dictionary. Write the number of the meaning that was used in the sentence.

1. Do you know the ___*right*___ answer?   1

2. We should buy a ___ for this dark room.

3. The waterfall was a beautiful ___ .

4. Ann throws the ball with her ___ hand.

5. That ___ boy answered every question.

6. The blind man regained his ___ .

7. The candle gave off a soft ___ .

8. That spotlight is very ___ .

high	night	right	might	tonight
sigh	sight	light	bright	frighten
thigh	fight	tight	flight	lightning

Build Word Power

Make new words by adding endings to your spelling words. You do not need to change the base word in any way before you add an ending.

s ed ing er est

high
(2 words)

night
(1 word)

bright
(2 words)

sigh
(3 words)

fight
(3 words)

light
(5 words)

frighten
(3 words)

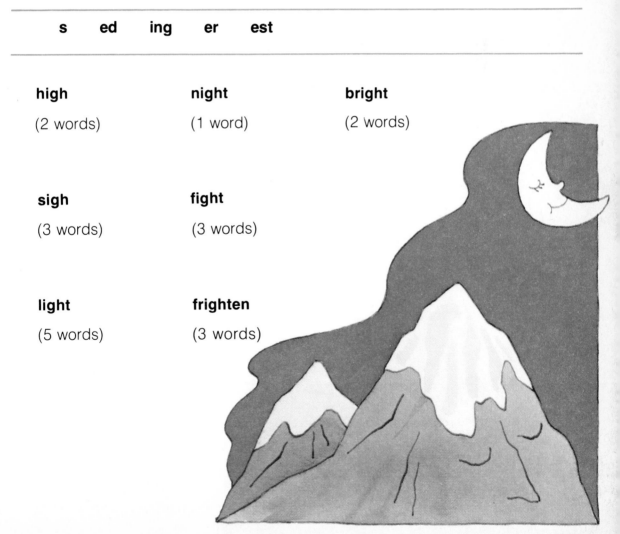

New Words   height   midnight   twilight
                 slight   delighted

Reach Out for New Words

A Beginning with the spelling word **light**, follow the directions to
make the five new **igh** words.

Look at the word **light**.

1. Add **s** to the beginning.

2. Change **s** to **twi**.

3. Change **twi** to **de**.
   Add **ed** to the end.

4. Take away **ed**.
   Change **del** to **midn**.

5. Change **midn** to **he**.

Proofreading

B Find the five misspelled words. Write the words correctly.

*It was twiligt when a sleight
rain began. Bill was delited
to hear the raindrops on the roof.
The weatherman had said there would be a
bad storm. The storm would be at its
hight around midnite.*

19.
storm
story
word

20.
very
every
summer

21.
pitch   pitcher
skate   skater
win   winner

22.
wind   windy
ice   icy
fun   funny

23.
heavy   heavier   heaviest
large   larger   largest
big   bigger   biggest

24.
wear
learn
hear

25.
right
high
light

A Look at the first pair of words in each row. In what way do these words go together? Write a spelling word that makes the second pair of words go together in the same way as the first pair.

1. **storm** is to **stormy**   as   **wind** is to ____

2. **bravest** is to **brave**   as   **largest** is to ____

3. **swim** is to **swimmer**   as   **win** is to ____

4. **dance** is to **dancer**   as   **skate** is to ____

5. **stormy** is to **storm**   as   **windy** is to ____

6. **windy** is to **windier**   as   **heavy** is to ____

7. **swimmer** is to **swim**   as   **winner** is to ____

8. **happiest** is to **happy**   as   **funniest** is to ____

Proofreading

B Find each misspelled word. Write the words correctly on your paper.

1. *Verry few skaters were on the icey pond.*
(2 words)

2. *I can lern to spell everey word right.*
(2 words)

3. *The stoarm blew down the largist tree.*
(2 words)

C Find the word from the box that goes in each blank.

story	*hear*	*right*	*summer*	*word*
pitcher	*light*	*wear*	*high*	*biggest*

1. a spelling ___

2. ___ your coat

3. baseball ___

4. write a ___

5. my ___ hand

6. the ___ piece

7. ___ as a feather

8. ___ in the air

9. hot ___ day

10. ___ a noise

A Write the fifteen words on your paper. Then follow these directions.

1. Put a ☐ around each **silent e** word.
Write the **er** form of these words.

2. Put a ⬭ around each **consonant + y** word.
Write the **er** form of these words.

3. Put a * after each **1 + 1 + 1 word.**
Write the **er** form of these words.

4. Write the **er** form of the four words you have left.

1. shop	**6.** fly	**11.** carry
2. ☐ brave ☐ *braver*	**7.** large	**12.** bake
3. dark	**8.** dance	**13.** copy
4. lead	**9.** small	**14.** wipe
5. hot	**10.** swim	**15.** work

B Three words in each row follow the same spelling pattern. One does not. Find that word. Be ready to tell why it does not belong.

1. sleepiest   darkest   windiest   luckiest

2. saddest   hottest   biggest   largest

3. bear   earn   clear   fight

4. world   herd   person   very

5. smoky   shady   salty   shiny

6. swim   worm   shop   win

7. right   large   bright   high

C Look at the first pair of words in each row. Write a word from the box that makes the second pair of words go together in the same way.

sandy	sight	painter	night
horn	winter	bright	fork

1. **light** is to **day**   as   **dark** is to _____

2. **beat** is to **drum**   as   **blow** is to _____

3. **pen** is to **writer**   as   **brush** is to _____

4. **soup** is to **spoon**   as   **meat** is to _____

5. **lawn** is to **grassy**   as   **beach** is to _____

6. **ears** are to **hearing**   as   **eyes** are to _____

7. **dark** is to **light**   as   **dull** is to _____

8. **hot** is to **summer**   as   **cold** is to _____

melted	from	minutes	always
month	drift	warning	during
also	flood	forecast	evening
warm	burst	beautiful	almost

Prewriting. Prewriting means getting ready to write. You must plan and organize your ideas before you begin writing.

Use Prewriting Skills

Use the spelling words to plan a report about the weather.

1. What two words can you use to describe the weather?
2. What two words remind you of snow?
3. What is caused by too much rain or melted snow?
4. What two words are measures of time?
5. What word means to tell about something before it happens?

Now Think

Pretend you are a weather reporter. Will you tell about an awful storm or about a beautiful day? Think about a time when the weather was really special for some reason. What kinds of things happened because of the weather? On your own paper, write some ideas for a weather report.

Writing. A story may be made up of paragraphs. A paragraph is a group of sentences about one idea. Each sentence in a paragraph tells about that main idea. The sentences must be arranged in an order that makes sense.

Use Writing Skills

A Practice writing topic sentences that tell a main idea. Write two different endings for each sentence starter below.

1. Today's weather was the ____ .

2. Everyone was surprised by ____ .

Sometimes two parts of the same sentence are incorrectly separated by a period. One part is not a complete thought. It must be joined to the rest of the sentence.

Incomplete: I ran into the house. Because it started to rain.

Complete: I ran into the house because it started to rain.

B Make each word group into a complete sentence. Write the sentences on your own paper.

1. a beautiful summer day

2. almost melted

3. a sudden burst of rain

4. earlier this evening

5. swept away by flood water

6. during a winter storm

7. a few minutes later

8. a warning to drivers

Now Write   Write a first draft of your paragraph about the weather. Follow the directions below.

1. Begin with a topic sentence. You may want to use one of the topic sentences from Exercise A.

2. Try to use some of the sentences from Exercise B. Put your sentences in an order that makes sense. First tell about the weather. Next, tell what happens because of the weather. Then give a forecast of the coming weather.

Revising. Revising means changing parts of your first draft to make it better. First read your draft aloud to make sure that you like the way your ideas sound. Then proofread your writing to find mistakes in capitalization, punctuation, and spelling.

Use Revising and Proofreading Skills

A Revise the ideas in the report below. Copy the revised story on your own paper.

1. Find a sentence in the first paragraph that would be better at the end of the story. It tells about tomorrow's weather.
2. Find a sentence that has a missing word. Find another sentence that is an incomplete thought. Add the needed words.
3. In the third paragraph, find a sentence that doesn't tell about the main idea.

Last night's snowstorm took everyone by surprise. The snow is expected to melt by tomorrow. Snow has never fallen in Janesville so late in the spring. May is the month when winter is supposed to over!

Yesterday was beautiful. The sun felt warm and spring was in the air. A few flowers were beginning to bud. Chirping in the trees. Children carried their jackets home from school in the afternoon.

During the night, though, winter came back without warning. Snow and ice covered the ground. Since no one was ready to clear the roads this morning, school buses couldn't travel and schools were closed. Janesville bought two new school buses last year.

B Practice your proofreading skills. Find the mistakes and rewrite the story correctly.

1. Find out eight misspelled words and write them correctly.
2. Find and correct six capitalization mistakes.
3. Find and correct four punctuation errors.

Remember
- A sentence begins with a capital letter and ends with a period.
- The names of particular places are capitalized.
- A period is not used to separate parts of one thought.

Today was the hottest day of the summer in downtown columbus. July is allways a warm mounth in our City, but today's heat was awful. The sun beat down frum the cloudless sky. The streets were quiet. Because no one wanted to be out in the bright sun. A boy came out of the Favorite flavor Factory with an ice cream cone in his hand. Two minits later, his ice cream had meltid. And dripped on the hot sidewalk. Durring the afternoon, a few clouds drifted across the sky? They didn't make it any cooler, though. The weather forcast for tomorrow is not much better, it will be all most as hot as today.

Now Revise Read the first draft of your story. Is each sentence about the main idea? Are the sentences arranged in an order that makes sense? Proofread and correct mistakes in capitalization, punctuation, and spelling. Write your final copy in your best handwriting.

A Writer's Journal

UNIT FOUR

Has a poem ever made you think, "This is how I feel" or "*I've done these things*"? A poem may help you remember happy times or sad times you may have had with a friend or with your family. That's why reading poetry is one way to get ideas for writing in your journal.

Read this poem. Try to picture in your mind what the two friends are doing. Then discuss the questions with your class.

SECRET TALK

I have a friend
and sometimes we meet
and greet each other
without a word.

We walk through a field
and stalk a bird
and chew a blade of
pungent grass.

We let time pass
for a golden hour
while we twirl a flower
of Queen Ann's lace
or find a lion's face
shaped in a cloud
that's drifting, sifting
across the sky.

There's no need to say,
"It's been a fine day"
when we say goodbye:
when we say goodbye
we just wave a hand
and we understand.

—EVE MERRIAM

Talking About the Poem

1. Where are the two friends playing? What are some of the things the two friends did?

2. Why don't the friends need to say that it had been a fine day when they say goodbye?

3. What is "secret talk"?

Writing in Your Journal

The poem talks about two friends. Maybe this poem has helped you remember a special friend and has given you an idea to write about in your journal. If you need help getting started, here are some other ideas you might use.

1. Write about some special looks, actions, or words that you and a friend use and understand.

2. Write about a special time that you and a friend had together. Describe where you were and what you did.

Building a Personal Word List

You have been collecting your misspelled words and writing them on your personal word list. How can you learn to spell these words? You might try one of these ways:

1. Look carefully at the words on your list. Do any of them look like words you already know how to spell? For example, knowing how to spell **grimy** may help you spell **slimy**.

2. Look for patterns. Do any of your words have spelling patterns you know? For example, you might notice that **high, bright,** and **lightning** have the same **igh** pattern. Practice spelling the words as a group.

wrist	*wrist*
wrong	*wrong*
wreck	*wreck*
wren	*wren*
wrapper	*wrapper*
knee	*knee*
know	*know*
knew	*knew*
knuckle	*knuckle*
knotted	*knotted*
climb	*climb*
comb	*comb*
crumb	*crumb*
lamb	*lamb*
limb	*limb*

1. What silent letter begins each word in the first group?
2. What silent letter begins each word in the second group?
3. What silent letter ends each word in the third group?

Some words are spelled with a silent letter.

Practice the Words

A Write the spelling words that complete this story.

   Carol didn't __1__ how much fun her uncle's

farm could be. She fed a young __2__ milk from a

bottle. She gave a baby duck a __3__ of bread.

   Next, Carol was allowed to __4__ on a pony's

back and take a ride. Her uncle told her to wrap

the reins around her hand. She learned to guide

the pony by moving her __5__ or her __6__. At first

Carol did it all __7__. She thought she would __8__

the corral! Soon she __9__ what to do. When the

ride was over, she __10__ the reins around a fence

post. Her uncle let her __11__ the pony's mane.

Then she fed the pony pieces of apple.

B Write the spelling word that rhymes with the clue word.

1. hen

2. spotted

3. go

4. slam

5. trim

6. two

7. gum

8. snapper

9. time

10. buckle

Dictionary

The dictionary gives many clues to explain the meanings of words.
The dictionary may give a sample sentence to make the meaning clearer.
The dictionary may give a picture of the word.

know (nō) *verb* to be aware of; realize [Does he *know* what happened?] —**knew, known, know' ing**

lamb (lam) *noun* a young sheep. —*plural* **lambs**

C Make two columns on your paper as shown below. Look up each word in your spelling dictionary. Write it in the correct column.

know limb knee   wrong wreck wren
lamb comb wrapper wrist climb knuckle

Sentence Clue

know

(5 words)

Picture Clue

lamb

(7 words)

148

wrist	wren	know	knotted	crumb
wrong	wrapper	knew	climb	lamb
wreck	knee	knuckle	comb	limb

Build Word Power

Follow the directions to change each clue word into a spelling word.

Clue Word	Change	Spelling Word
1. lime	**e** to **b**	*limb*
2. twist	**tw** to **wr**	
3. trapper	**t** to **w**	
4. crust	**st** to **mb**	
5. blew	**bl** to **kn**	
6. wrote	**te** to **ng**	
7. click	**ck** to **mb**	
8. knot	*t to w*	know
9. lamp		lamb
10. free		knee
11. check		wreck
12. chuckle		knuckle

Search for new words!
Follow the directions below.

Reach Out for New Words

A Find the correct path through this maze. You are on the right path if you pass words that have a silent letter. Write the eight words from your path.

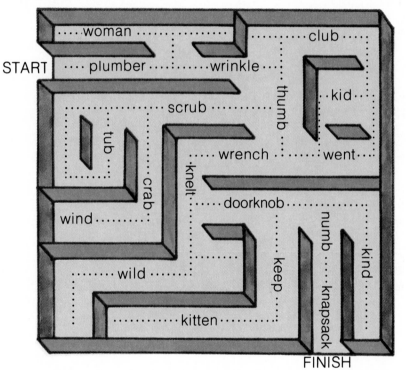

B Find the misspelled word in each group. Write the word correctly.

1. crumb
wrong
plumer
knew

2. rinkle
comb
wreck
knapsack

3. wrong
doornob
lamb
know

4. wreck
know
wrist
thum

5. wrapper
knotted
num
knee

6. rench
limb
knelt
climb

un +	true	=	untrue	*untrue*
un +	fair	=	unfair	*unfair*
un +	kind	=	unkind	*unkind*
un +	wise	=	unwise	*unwise*
un +	safe	=	unsafe	*unsafe*
un +	tie	=	untie	*untie*
un +	lock	=	unlock	*unlock*
un +	cover	=	uncover	*uncover*
un +	wrap	=	unwrap	*unwrap*
un +	plug	=	unplug	*unplug*
un +	pack	=	unpack	*unpack*
un +	button	=	unbutton	*unbutton*
un +	willing	=	unwilling	*unwilling*
un +	even	=	uneven	*uneven*
un +	opened	=	unopened	*unopened*

A **prefix** is a group of letters added to the beginning of a word to change its meaning.

1. What prefix was added to each base word to make the words in the last column?
2. Was the spelling of the base word changed when the prefix was added?

The prefix **un** means not or opposite of.
Do not change the spelling of the base word when you add the prefix **un**.
   un + happy = unhappy or **not happy**

151

untrue   unwise   unlock   unplug   unwilling

unfair   unsafe   uncover   unpack   uneven

unkind   untie   unwrap   unbutton   unopened

Practice the Words

A Use each clue to find a spelling word that fits in the puzzle.

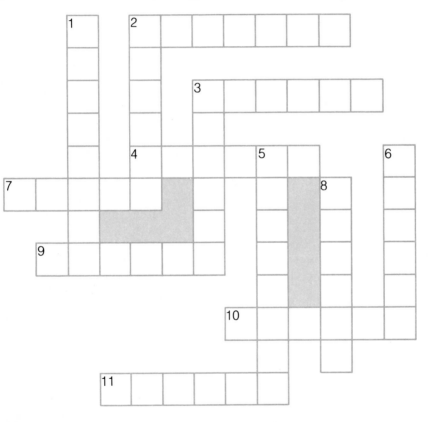

Across
2. to take the lid off
3. not playing by the rules
4. to pull out a plug
7. _____ your shoelaces
9. _____ the door
10. dangerous
11. not nice

Down
1. to loosen buttons
2. false
3. to take clothes from a suitcase
5. closed
6. foolish
8. to take off wrapping paper

B In each sentence, find the base form of one of your spelling words. Add the prefix **un** to the word. You will make a word with the opposite meaning.

1. Bill told a true story.

2. Julie said the test was fair.

3. We should cover the wet clay.

4. Remember to tie your shoe.

5. The hem of the skirt was even.

6. I am willing to wash the dishes.

Dictionary

Many words with prefixes are listed as entry words in the dictionary.

C Write your spelling words in alphabetical order. When words begin with the same letter, look at the next letter to find the alphabetical order. For some words, you will need to look at the third, fourth, or fifth letter.

unload

unlock

unlucky

untrue	unwise	unlock	unplug	unwilling
unfair	unsafe	uncover	unpack	uneven
unkind	untie	unwrap	unbutton	unopened

Build Word Power

Find the spelling word that completes each sentence. Change the spelling word to a form that will make sense in the sentence. Then write the word. You may add endings such as **s**, **ed**, or **ing**. You may also take off the prefix **un**. Watch out for **silent e** and **1 + 1 + 1** words.

1. Sue unpack her suitcase when she got home.   _unpacked_

2. It is unwise to look both ways before you cross the street.

3. Becky enjoys unwrap her birthday gifts.

4. Bill unbutton his coat when the cold wind began to blow.

5. Betty uncover the pot and cooks the rice.

New Words	unhurt	unhealthy	unafraid	unable
	unbroken	unfasten	unequal	unripe

Reach Out for New Words

A Unscramble each new word. First find the prefix **un**, which is not
scrambled. Then unscramble the rest of the letters. Write each
new word.

1. nesuntaf   5. preiun

2. lunaque   6. teaunhylh

3. truhun   7. draifuna

4. blunea   8. nebkunor

B Write the new **un** word that means the same as each word or
phrase below.

1. sick   5. brave

2. all in one piece   6. not the same

3. to open buttons   7. not ready to eat

4. not able to   8. not in pain

re + write = rewrite *rewrite*
re + fill = refill *refill*
re + read = reread *reread*
re + paint = repaint *repaint*
re + pay = repay *repay*
re + wind = rewind *rewind*
re + visit = revisit *revisit*
re + heat = reheat *reheat*
re + teach = reteach *reteach*
re + build = rebuild *rebuild*
re + tell = retell *retell*
re + turn = return *return*
re + take = retake *retake*
re + print = reprint *reprint*
re + place = replace *replace*

1. What prefix was added to each base word to make the words in the last column?
2. Was the spelling of the base word changed before the prefix was added?

The prefix **re** means <u>again</u> or <u>back</u>.
Do not change the spelling of the base word when you add the prefix **re**.
   re + paint = **repaint** or **paint again**

A Change the underlined words in each sentence to one spelling word.

1. Please <u>fill</u> my glass <u>again</u>.

2. Ms. Gomez will <u>teach</u> the lesson <u>again</u>.

3. Will you <u>tell</u> my favorite story <u>again</u>?

4. Ken should <u>pay</u> <u>back</u> the quarter he owes you.

5. Val wants to <u>paint</u> her room <u>again</u>.

6. They are going to <u>build</u> the clubhouse <u>again</u>.

7. Should I <u>take</u> your picture <u>again</u>?

8. Did you <u>write</u> your story <u>again</u>?

9. I will <u>heat</u> the soup <u>again</u> for lunch.

10. Today we must <u>turn</u> <u>back</u> our library books.

11. Jerry will <u>wind</u> the toy robot <u>again</u>.

12. Our class will <u>visit</u> the museum <u>again</u>.

rewrite	repaint	revisit	rebuild	retake
refill	repay	reheat	retell	reprint
reread	rewind	reteach	return	replace

B Look at each word. If it is spelled correctly, draw a ☺. If it is misspelled, write the word correctly.

1. retell

2. reheet

3. replase

4. rewrite

5. rebild

6. revissit

7. repprint

8. refil

9. rereed

10. reteach

11. retern

12. repay

Dictionary

C The words below are dictionary guide words. Write the spelling words that would appear on the same page.

1. retain/revote
(5 words)

2. rewash/rezone
(2 words)

3. repaid/rerun
(5 words)

Build Word Power

Make four new words from each base word below. Add the prefix **re** or one of the endings shown in the train. Sometimes you may want to use both a prefix and an ending. Watch out for **silent e** words.

re | Base Word | s | es | ed | ing | er

---

1. write	2. paint	3. teach
rewrite	—	—
writer	—	—
writing	—	—
rewrites	—	—

4. build	5. fill	6. read
—	—	—
—	—	—
—	—	—
—	—	—

Reach Out for New Words

A Print the **re** form of the new word that fits in each shape.

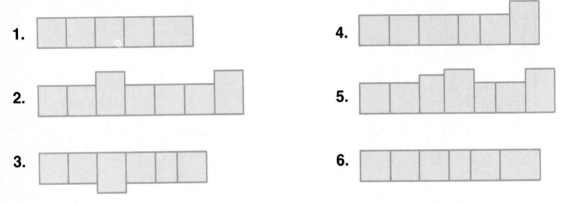

1.
2.
3.

4.
5.
6.

B Write the **re** form of each new word in alphabetical order. Then look up each word in your spelling dictionary and complete the definition.

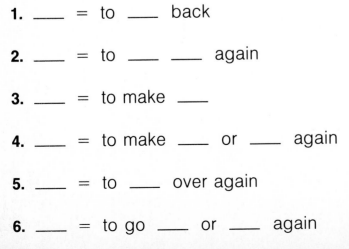

1. ___ = to ___ back

2. ___ = to ___ ___ again

3. ___ = to make ___

4. ___ = to make ___ or ___ again

5. ___ = to ___ over again

6. ___ = to go ___ or ___ again

let +	us	=	let's	*let's*
are +	not	=	aren't	*aren't*
did +	not	=	didn't	*didn't*
do +	not	=	don't	*don't*
was +	not	=	wasn't	*wasn't*
were +	not	=	weren't	*weren't*
I +	have	=	I've	*I've*
you +	have	=	you've	*you've*
that +	is	=	that's	*that's*
how +	is	=	how's	*how's*
what +	is	=	what's	*what's*
who +	is	=	who's	*who's*
he +	will	=	he'll	*he'll*
we +	will	=	we'll	*we'll*
we +	are	=	we're	*we're*

1. The words in the last column are **contractions**.
   Each contraction is made from how many words?
2. Were any letters left out when the words were put together?
3. In each contraction, an **apostrophe** takes the
   place of one or more letters. Draw an apostrophe.

A **contraction** is made from two words. When the two words are put
together, an **apostrophe (')** takes the place of one or more letters.

let's	don't	I've	how's	he'll
aren't	wasn't	you've	what's	we'll
didn't	weren't	that's	who's	we're

Practice the Words

A Make three columns on your paper as shown below.
Write the contractions in alphabetical order in the first column.
Answer the questions at the top of the second and third columns.

	Contraction	What two words is it made from?	What letter(s) does the ' replace?
1.	*aren't*	*are not*	*o*
2.	—	—	—
3.	—	—	—
4.	*he'll*	—	—
5.	—	—	—
6.	—	—	—
7.	—	—	—
8.	—	—	—
9.	—	—	—
10.	—	—	*wi*
11.	—	—	—
12.	—	—	—
13.	—	—	—
14.	—	—	—
15.	—	—	—

B Match the words with the correct endings to make contractions. Write each contraction you make.

1. what
2. do
3. are   ___ **'s**
4. how   ___ **n't**
5. you   ___ **'ve**
6. I
7. were

C Read each sentence. Find each pair of words that can be made into a contraction. Write the contraction.

1. We are sure we will enjoy the game.
   (2 contractions)

2. Carol was not singing because she did not know the song.
   (2 contractions)

3. That is the record he will bring to the party.
   (2 contractions)

4. Let us ask Mary who is going to the game.
   (2 contractions)

let's	don't	I've	how's	he'll
aren't	wasn't	you've	what's	we'll
didn't	weren't	that's	who's	we're

Build Word Power

Writing

Write a sentence to answer each question. In your answer, use the contraction in parentheses. Remember to start each sentence with a capital letter.

1. What is Fred going to do this weekend?   (he'll)

2. What books have you read this year?   (I've)

3. When will we pick up Jean at the airport?   (we'll)

4. What shall we have for dinner?   (let's)

5. Why didn't you finish your homework?   (don't)

6. How many cookies are in the cookies jar?   (aren't)

couldn't   shouldn't   hasn't   doesn't   hadn't
           I'd   you'd   they'd   she'd   we'd

Reach Out for New Words

A Write the contraction for each pair of words. Each contraction
   should fit in the boxes. An apostrophe fills one box.

1. she would

2. they would

3. does not

4. you would

5. could not

6. I would

7. has not

8. we would

9. had not

Proofreading

B Find each misspelled word. Write the word correctly.

1. They'ed already finished the job.
2. I thought youd like a snack.
3. That lamp dosen't work.
4. Could't we wait inside?
5. Here's the book Id like to read.

165

The possessive form of nouns

man	man's	*man's*
woman	woman's	*woman's*
girl	girl's	*girl's*
boy	boy's	*boy's*
mother	mother's	*mother's*
father	father's	*father's*
brother	brother's	*brother's*
sister	sister's	*sister's*
grandmother	grandmother's	*grandmother's*
grandfather	grandfather's	*grandfather's*
aunt	aunt's	*aunt's*
uncle	uncle's	*uncle's*
cousin	cousin's	*cousin's*
baby	baby's	*baby's*
child	child's	*child's*

The **possessive form** of a noun shows that something belongs to someone.

1. Each noun in the first column names a _____.
2. The nouns in the second column are in the possessive form. What was added to each noun?
3. Was the spelling of the base word changed before **'s** was added?

Make the **possessive form** of a noun by adding **'s**.
Do not change the spelling of the base word before adding **'s**.
That car belongs to my father. That is my father's car.

Writing

A Choose something from the box that can belong to each person listed below. Then write a phrase using both words. Use the correct possessive form for each person.

football	*house*	*pen*	*kitten*	*desk*
balloon	*dog*	*ring*	*socks*	*shorts*
radio	*hat*	*jacket*	*boat*	*car*

1. aunt   *my aunt's kitten*

2. boy   **9.** father

3. cousin   **10.** girl

4. woman   **11.** baby

5. uncle   **12.** brother

6. mother   **13.** grandmother

7. man   **14.** child

8. sister   **15.** grandfather

B Find the misspelled word in each group. Write the word correctly.

1. woman's
   father's
   brother's
   cuosin's

2. mother's
   babie's
   sister's
   girl's

3. aunt's
   uncle's
   mans'
   boy's

4. uncel's
   grandfather's
   aunt's
   mother's

5. father's
   boy's
   sister's
   chileds'

6. girl's
   grandmother's
   bruther's
   woman's

C Words are written in two directions in this puzzle. → ↓ Find the base form of nine spelling words. Then write the possessive form of each.

```
g  i  r  l  g  f  g
r  c  z  h  x  a  r
a  u  n  t  b  t  a
n  k  f  j  w  h  n
d  b  l  v  t  e  d
m  o  t  h  e  r  f
o  y  b  m  a  b  a
t  d  m  g  r  l  t
h  w  o  m  a  n  h
e  n  h  p  i  q  e
r  s  i  s  t  e  r
```

man's	mother's	grandmother's	cousin's
woman's	father's	grandfather's	baby's
girl's	brother's	aunt's	child's
boy's	sister's	uncle's	

Build Word Power

Rewrite each sentence using the possessive form of the underlined word.

1. This dog belongs to my <u>sister</u>.

This is my sister's dog.

2. This glove belongs to the <u>boy</u>.

3. Mr. Kim is a neighbor of my <u>uncle</u>.

4. Tess is a friend of my <u>brother</u>.

5. Mrs. Sill is the teacher of my <u>cousin</u>.

6. These golf clubs belong to my <u>aunt</u>.

New Words doctor nephew lady niece
nurse neighbor friend daughter

Reach Out for New Words

A Add the missing letters to make the new words.
Write the word. Then write its possessive form.

1. ___ ur ___ ___

2. ___ eigh ___ ___ ___

3. ___ ___ dy

4. ___ ie ___ ___

5. ___ ___ ie ___ ___

6. ___ ___ ___ ___ or

7. ___ ___ ph ___ ___

8. ___ augh ___ ___ ___

B Write a phrase using each pair of words. Use the possessive form
of each new word.

1. lady   umbrella   *the lady's umbrella*

2. nurse   uniform

3. doctor   office

apple	*apple*
puzzle	*puzzle*
little	*little*
bottle	*bottle*
rattle	*rattle*
middle	*middle*
wiggle	*wiggle*
bubble	*bubble*
puddle	*puddle*
juggle	*juggle*
scribble	*scribble*
cattle	*cattle*
nibble	*nibble*
riddle	*riddle*
giggle	*giggle*

1. How many words have the letters **tt**?   **gg**?   **bb**?   **dd**?

2. What other double letters do you see?

3. Are the double letters in each word vowels or consonants?

4. What two letters come after each double consonant?

Many words have a **double consonant** followed by **le**.

A Write the word that fits each clue.

1. I'm the center.

2. I'm all wet and shaped like .

3. I float through the air.

4. I'm very small.

5. Can you find an answer to me?

6. Babies like to play with me.

7. I'm a cute laugh.

8. Put me together to make this shape: .

9. I'm a little bite.

10. I'm shaped like .

11. You write me and I'm shaped like .

12. I'm made of glass.

13. I'm the way a worm moves.

apple	bottle	wiggle	juggle	nibble
puzzle	rattle	bubble	scribble	riddle
little	middle	puddle	cattle	giggle

B Complete the funny answers for these clues with two rhyming spelling words.

1. shake the cows   ___ the ___

2. twist and turn when you laugh ___ and ___

3. the joke in the center   ___ in the ___

4. chew on messy writing   ___ the ___

apple   puzzle   little   bottle
bubble   puddle   juggle

C Write the words from the box in alphabetical order. Then look up each word in your spelling dictionary. Divide it into syllables. Write **SC** if there is a sentence clue in the dictionary. Write **PC** if there is a picture clue.

1. ___apple___   ___ap·ple___

Writing

Write a sentence with each group of spelling words. You may add the endings **s, ed, ing, y, er,** and **est**. Remember that all your spelling words end with a silent **e**!

1. nibble, apple, cattle

2. bubble, puddle, middle

3. bottle, juggle, giggle

4. little, wiggle, rattle

Reach Out for New Words

A Words are printed in three directions in this puzzle. → ↓ ↘ Find and write each new word.

s	d	r	i	b	b	l	e
e	a	t	c	a	b	r	f
t	q	d	u	t	c	s	i
t	d	b	d	t	n	p	d
l	g	f	d	l	w	v	d
e	l	k	l	e	e	m	l
h	j	k	e	t	t	l	e
h	u	d	d	l	e	x	z

B Find the word in each sentence that does not make sense. Replace that word with a new word that rhymes with it.

1. Terry plays the riddle.
2. Help me put the paddle on my horse.
3. Scribble the basketball down the court.
4. Our toy soldiers fought a cattle.
5. I love to muddle the baby!
6. The football players met in a puddle.

air	+	plane	=	airplane	*airplane*
air	+	port	=	airport	*airport*
out	+	side	=	outside	*outside*
in	+	side	=	inside	*inside*
up	+	stairs	=	upstairs	*upstairs*
bed	+	room	=	bedroom	*bedroom*
class	+	room	=	classroom	*classroom*
after	+	noon	=	afternoon	*afternoon*
week	+	end	=	weekend	*weekend*
some	+	times	=	sometimes	*sometimes*
an	+	other	=	another	*another*
any	+	thing	=	anything	*anything*
may	+	be	=	maybe	*maybe*
break	+	fast	=	breakfast	*breakfast*
out	+	fit	=	outfit	*outfit*

1. The words in the last column are **compound words**.
   Each compound word is made from how many smaller words?
2. Did the spellings of the smaller words change when they were put together?

A **compound word** is made from two smaller words.
Do not change the spellings of the words when you put them together

A Write the spelling words that complete the story.

My friend Tommy once flew on a jet ___. Now he loves

planes. At school I ___ see him staring out the window of our ___ .

He is watching the planes land at the nearby ___ .

Last ___ Tommy's parents took us to the airport. First we

went to the snack shop ___ the terminal building. We ate ___ .

Then we went ___ and climbed ___ to the observation deck.

We watched one jet after another take off or land.

Since Tommy loves planes so much, ___ he will become a

pilot! I can't think of anything he'd like better!

Proofreading

B Find the misspelled words. Write the words correctly.

1. *Do you have enough money to buy anuther outfit?*
(2 words)

2. *The areplane lands late this aftrenoon.*
(2 words)

3. *Take your costume upstares to your bedroome.*
(2 words)

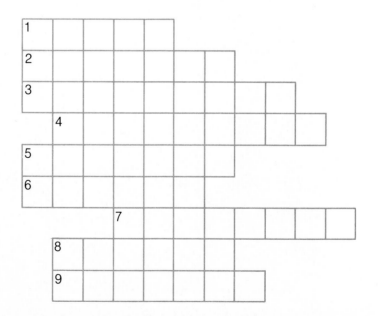

C Use each clue to find a spelling word that fits in the puzzle.

1. perhaps

2. a place to sleep

3. once in a while

4. where students learn

5. Saturday and Sunday

6. clothes you wear

7. something

8. opposite of **outside**

9. opposite of **inside**

airplane   upstairs   weekend   maybe
airport   bedroom   sometimes   breakfast
outside   classroom   another   outfit
inside   afternoon   anything

Build Word Power

Look at the first pair of words in each row. Write a word from the box that makes the second pair of words go together in the same way as the first pair.

1. **drive** is to **car**   as   **fly** is to _____

2. **train** is to **station**   as   **airplane** is to _____

3. **bottom** is to **top**   as   **downstairs** is to _____

4. **cook** is to **kitchen**   as   **sleep** is to _____

5. **seat** is to **bus**   as   **desk** is to _____

6. **A.M.** is to **morning**   as   **P.M.** is to _____

7. **Monday** is to **weekday**   as   **Sunday** is to _____

8. **grass** is to **outside**   as   **carpet** is to _____

Search for new words!
Follow the directions below.

Reach Out for New Words

A Rematch the word parts of these silly compounds to make real
compound words. Change only the underlined parts. Use each
word part once.

1. some<u>light</u>
2. basket<u>paper</u>
3. them<u>ground</u>
4. book<u>walk</u>
5. flash<u>fish</u>
6. rain<u>selves</u>
7. gold<u>ball</u>
8. side<u>mark</u>
9. play<u>one</u>
10. news<u>coat</u>

B Write the new word that might be found in each place.

1. in a bowl of water
2. between some pages
3. going through a net
4. in a dark room
5. out in a storm
6. next to the street

28.
wrapper
know
climb

29.
fair   unfair
tie   untie
lock   unlock

30.
paint   repaint
pay   repay
turn   return

32.
mother   mother's
father   father's
baby   baby's

31.
let us   let's
do not   don't
he will   he'll

33.
apple
puzzle
nibble

34.
upstairs
bedroom
afternoon

Using Review Words

A Look at the first pair of words in each row. Write a word from the box that makes the second pair of words go together in the same way as the first pair.

1. **paint** is to **repaint**   as   **pay** is to _____

2. **noon** is to **afternoon**   as   **room** is to _____

3. **let us** is to **let's**   as   **do not** is to _____

4. **untie** is to **tie**   as   **unlock** is to _____

5. **mother** is to **mother's**   as   **father** is to _____

6. **room** is to **bedroom**   as   **stairs** is to _____

7. **don't** is to **do not**   as   **he'll** is to _____

8. **tie** is to **untie**   as   **fair** is to _____

9. **father's** is to **father**   as   **baby's** is to _____

Proofreading

B Find the spelling mistakes. Then write each misspelled word correctly.

1. Let's reppaint our kitchen chairs this aftrenoon.
   (2 words)

2. This key will unlock my mothers suitcase.
   (1 word)

3. My pony likes to nible on a piece of appel.
   (2 words)

4. He'l retturn my watch tomorrow.
   (2 words)

C Complete each phrase with a word from the box.

puzzle	baby's	wrapper	climb
let's	know	untie	unlock

1. ___ the door

2. a candy ___

3. a crossword ___

4. ___ a ladder

5. ___ go out

6. ___ rattle

7. ___ the knot

8. ___ his name

A Use the directions following each base word to make another form of the word.

1. **write**   add prefix meaning **again**
2. **how**   form contraction using **is**
3. **kind**   add prefix meaning **not**
4. **true**   add prefix meaning **not**
5. **you**   form contraction using **have**
6. **opened**   add prefix meaning **not**
7. **man**   show possessive form
8. **that**   form contraction using **is**
9. **we**   form contraction using **will**
10. **girl**   show possessive form
11. **visit**   add prefix meaning **again**
12. **sister**   show possessive form
13. **willing**   add prefix meaning **not**
14. **uncle**   show possessive form
15. **we**   form contraction using **are**

B Three words in each row follow the same spelling pattern. One word does not. Find that word. Be ready to tell why it does not belong.

1. comb   sometimes   inside   another
2. outside   unpack   unplug   unbutton
3. knuckle   knee   knew   wreck
4. wasn't   aunt's   didn't   aren't
5. uncover   reread   lamb   uneven
6. who's   boy's   woman's   brother's
7. wrong   weekend   knee   crumb

C Look at the first pair of words in each row. Write a word from the box that makes the second pair of words go together in the same way as the first pair.

middle   wrist   wrong   little
unwrap   knee   unbutton

1. **shoe** is to **untie**   as   **shirt** is to ___

2. **elephant** is to **big**   as   **mouse** is to ___

3. **foot** is to **ankle**   as   **hand** is to ___

4. **head** is to **top**   as   **waist** is to ___

5. **spell** is to **misspell**   as   **right** is to ___

6. **arm** is to **elbow**   as   **leg** is to ___

7. **banana** is to **peel**   as   **gift** is to ___

twins	pair	closet	suitcase
fixed	gloves	trunk	stacked
hair	jacket	morning	woolen
worn	dresser	overslept	bedspread

Prewriting. Prewriting is thinking of ideas for a story. Writers plan their stories before they begin to write.

Use Prewriting Skills

Use the spelling words to write a story about twins going on a trip.

1. What two things can be worn?

2. What are four places to put clothes?

3. Which four words tell about actions that happened in the past?

4. Which three compound words might you use in your story?

Now Think   Think about twins getting ready to go on a trip. How old are they? Do they look alike or are they different? Are they going away for a weekend or for a long vacation? Think about the clothes they must pack. On your own paper, write some of your ideas for a story.

Writing. The people in a story are called **characters.** Writers must choose words that make the characters and the setting seem real.

Use Writing Skills

A Make each word group below into a good topic sentence. Each sentence should tell about twins who are going on a trip.

1. For weeks, Jerry and Jill ___ .

2. Today was finally the day when ___ .

Use good describing words to make a story seem real. Describing words paint a picture in your reader's mind.

Example: The bird was very strange. It had a tiny head and a huge beak. It had no neck at all. The body was round with short wings. Its long, thin legs were like stilts.

B Look at the describing words in each word group below. Then use each group in a complete sentence.

1. pair of warm, furry gloves

2. curly black hair

3. bright sunny morning

4. stuffed into the small suitcase

5. red woolen jacket

6. tall thin twins

Now Write   Write a first draft of your story.

1. Begin with a topic sentence. Do you want to use one of the sentences from Exercise A?

2. Try to use some of the sentences you wrote for Exercise B.

3. Use words that describe the characters and setting of your story.

Revising. Revising means changing parts of a first draft to make it better. First, revise your ideas. Then proofread for mistakes.

Use Revising and Proofreading Skills

A Revise this story. Then copy the revised story on your paper.

1. Find and correct two incomplete sentences.
2. Find two sentences with missing words. Find one sentence with two extra words.
3. Take out a sentence that doesn't fit the main idea.

Summertime had finally arrived. The Henley twins were almost ready for vacation. Leaving for the airport. The few things left to pack were stacked beside open suitcase.

"Nothing else will fit," groaned Shannon.

"No wonder," laughed Sharon. "There's nothing left in our closet! It looks as if we're going away for two years, not two months." She put two red woolen jackets back in the closet. Some other things in the dresser drawer.

Shannon said, "Leave our warm, furry gloves packed," Shannon said. "Canada is supposed to be cold." Canada is the second largest country in the world. Sharon snapped the suitcase closed.

"Wait!" Shannon yelled. "Where's the cat? She was sitting on the bedspread a minute ago." The twins looked at each other and started to laugh. Shannon opened the suitcase again. A frightened, furry white cat out onto the bed.

B Practice your proofreading skills on the story below. Find the six misspelled words. Find six punctuation errors and four capitalization errors. Rewrite the story correctly.

Remember
- Days of the week and proper names are capitalized.
- A period should not separate parts of one thought.
- A comma is used after each word in a series.
- An apostrophe is used in contractions.
- Quotation marks are used at the beginning and end of a speaker's words.

Tim and kim were going camping for the weekend. Kim was awake at five oclock Saturday morning. She had stacked everything she needed. On top of the dressar friday night. Now she packed in a hurry. Then she woke Tim, who always oversleped.

"Come on, sleepyhead," she said. Mom has fixt Breakfast for us already."

Tim kicked off his bedspred and jumped to his feet. He put on his jeans a jackett and an old pair of sneakers. He grabbed some clothes out of the closit and rolled them in his sleeping bag. Then he raced downstairs before Kim had finished eating.

"Come on, slowpoke, he said. "Do you want to make us late?"

Now Revise Read the first draft of your story. Are all the sentences complete? Did you use good describing words?
Proofread and correct mistakes in capitalization, punctuation, and spelling. Write the final copy of your story in your best handwriting.

Handbook

I. The Structure of Words

Syllables
Base Words
Prefixes
Word Endings
Contractions
Compound Words

II. The Function of Words

Nouns
Singular Nouns
Plural Nouns
Possessive Form of Nouns
Possessive Pronouns
Verbs
Past Tense Verbs
Adjectives

III. The Sound of Words

Vowels
Long Vowels
Short Vowels
Consonants
Silent Letters

Syllables

Words are made up of parts called syllables. The dictionary shows how words are divided into syllables.

>but·ter = two syllables
>dress = one syllable

Base Words
Base words are words before any changes have been made.

Base word	wrap
Base word with endings added	wrap<u>s</u> wrapp<u>ed</u> wrapp<u>ing</u>
Base word with prefix added	<u>un</u>wrap

Prefixes
A prefix is a syllable added to the beginning of a word to change the meaning.

>I wrapped the birthday present.
>(I put the paper on the present.)

>I <u>un</u>wrapped the birthday present.
>(I took the paper off the present.)

>I <u>re</u>wrapped the birthday present.
>(I put the paper back on the present.)

Word Endings

Word endings are letters added to the end of a word to change the way it is used.

play	Ryan will play ball.	(verb)
plays	Ryan plays ball.	(verb)
playing	Ryan is playing ball.	(verb)
played	Ryan played ball yesterday.	(past tense verb)
player	Ryan is a good player.	(noun)

Contractions

A contraction is made from two words. When the two words are put together, an apostrophe takes the place of one or more letters.

we are =	we **a**re	= we're
he will =	he **wi**ll	= he'll

Compound Words

A compound word is made from two smaller words. The spellings do not change when the words are put together.

class + room = classroom
after + noon = afternoon

II. The Function of Words means the way words are used.

Nouns

A noun is a word that names something.

> The <u>monkey</u> ate a <u>banana</u>.

The sentence has two words that are nouns.

Singular Nouns

A noun that names one thing is called a singular noun. The two nouns in this sentence are singular:

> The <u>monkey</u> ate a <u>banana</u>.
> (one monkey)   (one banana)

Plural Nouns

A noun that names more than one thing is a plural noun.

> The <u>monkeys</u> ate a banana.
> (more than one monkey)

> The monkey ate two <u>bananas</u>.
> (more than one banana)

Possessive Form of Nouns

The possessive form of a noun shows that something belongs to someone. Make the possessive form of a noun by adding **'s**.

> That car belongs to my father.
> That is my <u>father's</u> car.

Possessive Pronouns

A possessive pronoun takes the place of a noun in the possessive form.

My father's car = his car
The Clark's house = their house
Ashley's book = her book

A possessive pronoun is not spelled with an apostrophe.

Verbs

A verb is a word that tells about an action.

I walk on the beach in the summertime.
(Walk tells what I do.)

Past Tense Verbs

A verb that tells about an action that happened in the past is in the past tense.

We walked a mile to the beach.
We ran along the edge of the water.
(Walked and ran tell what we did.)

Adjectives

An adjective is a word that describes something.

We walked on the sandy beach.
(Sandy describes the beach.)

We ran into the cold water.
(Cold describes the water.)

Vowels
Five letters of the alphabet are called vowels. The vowels are **a**, **e**, **i**, **o**, and **u**.

Long Vowels
Long vowels are easy to hear because they "say their own names."

a	**e**	**i**	**o**	**u**
nation	me	fine	no	unit

Short Vowels
Short vowels sound like the vowels in these words:

a	**e**	**i**	**o**	**u**
at	ten	is	lot	up

Consonants
The consonants are all the letters of the alphabet except **a**, **e**, **i**, **o**, and **u**.

Silent Letters
Silent letters make no sound. You can see them in a word, but you cannot hear them.

Many words have a final silent **e**.

The last letter you see in the word hope is e.
The last letter you hear in the word hope is p.

Many words begin with a silent **k** or **w**.

The first letter you see in the word <u>knee</u> is <u>k</u>.
The first letter you hear in the word <u>knee</u> is <u>n</u>.

The first letter you see in the word <u>wrist</u> is <u>w</u>.
The first letter you hear in the word <u>wrist</u> is <u>r</u>.

Some words end with a silent **b**.

clim<u>b</u>   com<u>b</u>   lam<u>b</u>

Two letters are silent in the combination **igh**.
The letters **g** and **h** make no sound.

ri<u>gh</u>t   hi<u>gh</u>   li<u>gh</u>t

How To Find a Word

A dictionary is organized like a telephone book. It lists information in alphabetical order with guide words at the top of each page.

Guide Words

The guide words help you find the right page quickly. They tell you at a glance what section of the alphabet is included on each page. The guide word on the left tells you the first word on that page. The guide word on the right tells you the last word on that page. If the word you are looking for comes alphabetically between those two words, you are on the right page.

GUIDE WORDS

battle/bear
battle

bear

GUIDE WORDS

battle   **bear**
battle

bear

Alphabetical Order

Alphabetical order means the order of the letters in the alphabet.

Words beginning with **a** come first.   **a**bout

Words beginning with **b** come next.   **b**ear

Words beginning with **c** come   **c**lass
   after words beginning with **b**.

When two words begin with the same letter, you must look at the second letter of each word to determine alphabetical order. When several of the letters are the same, you will have to look at the third or fourth letter to determine the alphabetical order.

toa**d**   The first three letters in the words <u>toad</u> and <u>toast</u>
toa**st**   are the same. The fourth letter must be used to
       determine alphabetical order. Since **d** comes before
       s, <u>toad</u> is alphabetized before <u>toast</u>.

Words Listed

The words listed in a dictionary are called entry words. A word is usually listed in its base form. Other forms of the word may be listed within the same entry.

Word Forms	Base Form	Entry Word
hurrying hurried	hurry	hurry
dances dancing	dance	dance

What the Dictionary Tells About a Word

A dictionary tells you much more than the spelling and meaning of a word. The information it contains about each word is called the *entry*. The parts of an entry are labeled and explained below.

The ENTRY WORD is printed in heavy black type. It is divided into syllables.

A PICTURE may be used to help you understand the meaning of the entry word.

The PART OF SPEECH is shown after the pronunciation.

The RESPELLING tells you how to pronounce the word. The *Pronunciation Key* explains the respelling.

A STRESS MARK is placed after a syllable that gets an accent.

The DEFINITION is the meaning of the word. If a word has more than one meaning, each meaning is given a number.

OTHER FORMS of the entry word are included in the same entry.

A sample SENTENCE; can help you understand the meaning of the entry word.

mouse (mous) *noun*   a small, gnawing animal. —*plural* **mice**

mouth (mouth) *noun*   the opening in the head for eating and making sounds [The soup burned my *mouth*.] —*plural* **mouths**

move (mōōv) *verb*   **1** to change place or position [*Move* the picture to the left.] **2** to change the place where one lives [They *moved* to New York.] —**moved, mov′ ing**

mud·dy (mud′ ē) *adjective*   full of mud [Clean your *muddy* boots.] —**mud′ di·er, mud′ di·est**

mul·ti·ply (mul′ tə plī) *verb*   to repeat a figure a certain number of times [She *multiplied* 3 by 4 to get 12.] —**mul′ ti·plied, mul′ ti·ply·ing**

N

nap·kin (nap′ kin) *noun*   a piece of cloth or paper used while eating to protect clothes or to wipe fingers or lips. —*plural* **nap′ kins**

near (nir) *adjective*   not far; close [Our house is *near* to the school.] —**near′ er, near′ est**

neigh·bor (nā′ bər) *noun*   a person who lives near another. —*plural* **neigh′ bors**

Dictionary

Pronunciation Key

SYMBOL	KEY WORDS	SYMBOL	KEY WORDS	SYMBOL	KEY WORDS
a	ask, fat	u	up, cut	n	not, ton
ā	ape, date	ʉr	fur, fern	p	put, tap
ä	car, lot			r	red, dear
		ə	a in ago	s	sell, pass
e	elf, ten		e in agent	t	top, hat
er	berry, care		e in father	v	vat, have
ē	even, meet		i in unity	w	will, always
			o in collect	y	yet, yard
i	is, hit		u in focus	z	zebra, haze
ir	mirror, here				
ī	ice, fire			ch	chin, arch
		b	bed, dub	ng	ring, singer
ō	open, go	d	did, had	sh	she, dash
ô	law, horn	f	fall, off	th	thin, truth
oi	oil, point	g	get, dog	*th*	then, father
oo	look, pull	h	he, ahead	zh	s in pleasure
o͞o	ooze, tool	j	joy, jump		
yoo	unite, cure	k	kill, bake	'	as in (ā'b'l)
yoo	cute, few	l	let, ball		
ou	out, crowd	m	met, trim		

A heavy stress mark ' is placed after a syllable that gets a strong accent, as in **con·sid·er** (kən sid'ər).

A light stress mark ' is placed after a syllable that also gets an accent, but of a weaker kind, as in **dic·tion·ar·y** (dik'shən er'ē).

The dictionary definitions used throughout this book were specially prepared by the staff of McDougal, Littell & Company and are based upon the entries in *Webster's New World Dictionary for Young Readers* with the consent of the publisher of that work, Simon & Schuster, Inc.

A

a·ble (ā′ b'l) *adjective*　having the power to do something [She is *able* to take care of herself.] —**a′ bler, a′ blest**

a·bout (ə bout′) *preposition*　having to do with [This is a book *about* ships.]

a·corn (ā′ kôrn) *noun*　the nut of the oak tree. —*plural* **a′ corns**

a·cross (ə krôs′) *preposition*　from one side to the other [We swam *across* the river.]

ad·dress (ə dres′ *or* ad′ res) *noun*　the place where mail is sent. —*plural* **ad′ dress·es**

a·fraid (ə frād′) *adjective*　feeling fear [I'm *afraid* of the dark.]

af·ter·noon (af tər no͞on′) *noun*　the time of day from noon to evening. —*plural* **af·ter·noons′**

air·plane (er′ plān) *noun*　an aircraft driven forward by a jet engine or propeller. —*plural* **air′ planes**

air·port (er′ pôrt) *noun*　a place where aircraft take off and land. —*plural* **air′ ports**

all (ôl) *adjective*　the whole thing or amount [I have *all* the gold.]

al·ley (al′ ē) *noun*　a narrow street behind buildings [The garbage truck drove down the *alley*.] —*plural* **al′ leys**

al·most (ôl′ mōst) *adverb*　not completely; very nearly [He tripped and *almost* fell.]

al·so (ôl′ sō) *adverb*　in addition; too; besides [The man who directed the show *also* acted in it.]

al·ways (ôl′ wiz *or* ôl′ wāz) *adverb*　at all times [*Always* be courteous.]

A·mer·i·ca (ə mer′ ə kə) *noun*　North America or South America.

a·mount (ə mount′) *noun*　total [The bill was $50, but he paid only half that *amount*.]

an·oth·er (ə nu*th*′ ər) *adjective*　**1** one more [Take *another* apple.] **2** a different one [Exchange the book for *another* one.]

ant (ant) *noun*　a small insect that lives in or on the ground [Many *ants* crawled near our picnic.] —*plural* **ants**

an·y·thing (en′ ē thing) *pronoun*　any object, event, or fact [Did *anything* important happen today?]

ap·pear (ə pir′) *verb*　to come into sight [A ship *appeared* on the horizon.] —**ap·peared′, ap·pear′ ing**

ap·ple (ap′ 'l) *noun*　a round, firm fruit with green, yellow, or red skin. —*plural* **ap′ ples**

are·n't (ärnt)　are not [They *aren't* going.]

ar·gue (är′ gyōo) *verb*　quarrel [The children were *arguing* about whose turn it was.] —**ar′ gued, ar′ gu·ing**

ar·my (är′ mē) *noun*　a large group of soldiers. —*plural* **ar′ mies**

a·round (ə round′) *adverb*　in a circle [The wheel turned *around*.]

ar·row (ar′ ō) *noun*　a thin rod that is shot from a bow. —*plural* **ar′ rows**

ash (ash) *noun*　the powder left after something has burned. —*plural* **ash′ es**

ask (ask) *verb*　to use words in trying to find out [We *asked* how much it cost.] —**asked, ask′ ing**

a	fat	ir	here	ou	out	zh	leisure
ā	ape	ī	bite, fire	u	up	ng	ring
ä	car, lot	ō	go	ʉr	fur		a *in* ago
e	ten	ô	law, horn	ch	chin		e *in* agent
er	care	oi	oil	sh	she	ə =	i *in* unity
ē	even	oo	look	th	thin		o *in* collect
i	hit	o͞o	tool	*th*	then		u *in* focus

at·tic (at′ ik) *noun* the space just below the roof of a house. —*plural* **at′ tics**

aunt (ant or änt) *noun* a sister of one's mother or father. —*plural* **aunts**

aw·ful (ô′ fəl) *adjective* very bad, terrible; *used only in everyday talk* [The weather was *awful*.]

ax (aks) *noun* a tool for chopping wood [Lincoln split logs with an *ax*.] —*plural* **ax′ es**

B

ba·by (bā′ bē) *noun* infant. —*plural* **ba′ bies**

bag·gy (bag′ ē) *adjective* hanging loosely [The pants were *baggy* at the knees.] —**bag′ gi·er, bag′ gi·est**

bak·er (bāk′ ər) *noun* a person whose work is baking bread, cakes, and pastry. —*plural* **bak′ ers**

bak·er·y (bāk′ ər ē) *noun* a place where bread and cakes are baked or sold. —*plural* **bak′ er·ies**

ba·nan·a (bə nan′ ə) *noun* a large yellow fruit [Mother brought a bunch of *bananas*.] —*plural* **ba·nan′as**

bas·ket (bas′ kit) *noun* a container, often with handles [The apples were placed in a *basket*.] —*plural* **bas′ kets**

bas·ket·ball (bas′ kit bôl) *noun* a game played by two teams of five players.

bat·tle (bat′ ′l) *noun* warfare [He limps from a wound received in *battle*.] —*plural* **bat′ tles**

bay (bā) *noun* a part of a sea or lake that forms a curve in the coastline [The boat sailed across the *bay*.] —*plural* **bays**

bear (ber) *noun* a large, heavy animal with fur and a short tail. —*plural* **bears**

beard (bird) *noun* the hair growing on the lower part of a man's face. —*plural* **beards**

beau·ti·ful (byo͞ot′ ə fəl) *adjective* very pleasant to look at or hear [She has a *beautiful* face.]

bed (bed) *noun* furniture to sleep or rest on. —*plural* **beds**

bed·room (bed′ ro͞om) *noun* a room with a bed, for sleeping in. —*plural* **bed′ rooms**

bed·spread (bed′ spred) *noun* a cover spread over a bed when it is not being slept in. —*plural* **bed′ spreads**

bee (bē) *noun* an insect that has four wings and feeds on the nectar of flowers. —*plural* **bees**

beg (beg) *verb* to ask as a favor [She *begged* us not to tell the secret.] —**begged, beg′ ging**

ber·ry (ber′ ē) *noun* any small, juicy fruit with seeds. —*plural* **ber′ ries**

big (big) *adjective* large [That's a *big* dog.] —**big′ ger, big′ gest**

birth·day (burth′ dā) *noun* the day on which a person is born. —*plural* **birth′ days**

blan·ket (blang′ kit) *noun* a large cover to sit on or lie under [A picnic lunch was spread on the *blanket*.] —*plural* **blan′ kets**

blouse (blous) *noun* a garment like a shirt. —*plural* **blous′ es**

blue·jay (blo͞o′ jā) *noun* a bird with a blue back and feathers. —*plural* **blue′ jays**

boast (bōst) *verb* to brag or talk about with too much pride [He *boasted* about his bravery.] —**boast′ ed, boast′ ing**

boat (bōt) *noun* a small vessel used for traveling on water. —*plural* **boats**

bod·y (bäd′ ē) *noun* all parts of a person or animal. —*plural* **bod′ ies**

book·mark (book′ märk) *noun* something that marks a place in a book. —*plural* **book′ marks**

bore (bôr) *verb* to make tired by being dull [The speaker *bored* the crowd.] —**bored, bor′ ing**

born (bôrn) *a past form of* **bear**   given birth to [The twins were *born* an hour apart.]

both·er (bäth′ ər) *verb*   to annoy [Does the noise *bother* you?] —**both′ ered, both′ er·ing**

bot·tle (bät′ ′l) *noun*   a container usually made of glass or plastic [Get the *bottle* of milk.] —*plural* **bot′ tles**

bounce (bouns) *verb*   to hit against a surface so as to spring back [They *bounced* the ball against the wall.] —**bounced, bounc′ ing**

bound (bound) *verb*   to move with a leap or leaps [The dog came *bounding* to meet her.] —**bound′ ed, bound′ ing**

box (bäks) *noun*   a container used to hold or carry things in. —*plural* **box′ es**

boy (boi) *noun*   a male child. —*plural* **boys**

brag (brag) *verb*   to boast [She *bragged* about winning the race.] —**bragged, brag′ ging**

brave (brāv) *adjective*   full of courage; not afraid. —**brav′ er, brav′ est**

break·fast (brek′ fəst) *noun*   the first meal of the day.

breeze (brēz) *noun*   a light wind. —*plural* **breez′ es**

bright (brīt) *adjective*   **1** full of light [Some stars are very *bright*.] **2** clever [My brother is a *bright* child.] —**bright′ er, bright′ est**

bro·ken (brō′ kən) *adjective*   split into pieces [Pick up the *broken* dish.]

broth·er (bruth′ ər) *noun*   a boy or man as he is related to the other children of his parents. —*plural* **broth′ ers**

brush (brush) *noun*   a bunch of bristles fastened together for cleaning, painting, or grooming. —*plural* **brush′ es** ♦*verb*   to use a brush to clean, paint, or groom [*Brush* your teeth well.] —**brushed, brush′ ing**

bub·ble (bub′ ′l) *noun*   a thin film of liquid forming a ball around air [Look at the soap *bubbles*.] —*plural* **bub′ bles**

build (bild) *verb*   to make by putting together parts [Let's *build* a house.] —**built, build′ ing**

bun·ny (bun′ ē) *noun*   a rabbit. —*plural* **bun′ nies**

burn (bʉrn) *verb*   to be on fire [The candle *burned* brightly.] —**burned, burn′ ing**

burst (bʉrst) *verb*   to break open suddenly; explode [The balloon *burst* with a loud pop.] — **burst, burst′ ing**

bur·y (ber′ ē) *verb*   to put something under the ground [The dog *buried* its bone.] —**bur′ ied, bur′ y·ing**

bus (bus) *noun*   a large motor coach that carries passengers. —*plural* **bus′ es**

but·ter (but′ ər) *noun*   a spread for bread or cooking made by churning cream.

but·ter·fly (but′ ər flī) *noun*   an insect with four colorful wings. —*plural* **but′ ter·flies**

buy (bī) *verb*   to get by paying money [The Dutch *bought* Manhattan Island for about $24.] —**bought, buy′ ing**

C

cab·bage (kab′ ij) *noun*   a vegetable with thick leaves folded tightly to form a head [*Cabbage* may be eaten cooked or raw.] —*plural* **cab′ bag·es**

cage (kāj) *noun*   a closed-off space with wires or bars on the sides, in which to keep birds or animals. —*plural* **cag′ es**

a	fat	ir	here	ou	out	zh	leisure
ā	ape	ī	bite, fire	u	up	ng	ring
ä	car, lot	ō	go	ʉr	fur		a *in* ago
e	ten	ô	law, horn	ch	chin		e *in* agent
er	care	oi	oil	sh	she	ə =	i *in* unity
ē	even	oo	look	th	thin		o *in* collect
i	hit	o͞o	tool	th	then		u *in* focus

calf (kaf) *noun*   a young cow or bull. —*plural* **calves**

can·dy (kan′ dē) *noun*   a sweet food made from sugar or syrup. —*plural* **can′ dies**

car·ri·er (kar′ ē ər) *noun*   a person or thing that carries [A mail *carrier* delivered the package.] —*plural* **car′ ri·ers**

car·rot (kar′ ət) *noun*   a plant with a long, orange root eaten as a vegetable. —*plural* **car′ rots**

car·ry (kar′ ē) *verb*   to take from one place to another [Please help me *carry* these books upstairs.] —**car′ ried, car′ ry·ing**

catch (kach) *verb*   **1** to take hold of a person or thing that is moving [to *catch* a thief].   **2** to stop with the hands [to *catch* a ball]. —**caught, catch′ ing**

catch·er (kach′ ər) *noun*   in baseball, one who catches pitched balls not hit by the batter. —*plural* **catch′ ers**

cat·tle (kat′ ′l) *plural noun*   animals of the cow family raised on farms and ranches.

change (chānj) *verb*   to make or become different [She *changed* her mind.] —**changed, chang′ ing**

char·coal (chär′ kōl) *noun*   a form of carbon used as a fuel or filter.

chase (chās) *verb*   to follow in order to catch. —**chased, chas′ ing**

cher·ry (cher′ ē) *noun*   a small, round, red fruit. —*plural* **cher′ ries**

chess (ches) *noun*   a game played on a chessboard by two players.

child (chīld) *noun*   a young boy or girl. —*plural* **chil′ dren**

chill (chil) *noun*   a feeling of coldness [There was a *chill* in the air.] —*plural* **chills**

chim·ney (chim′ nē) *noun*   a pipe or shaft that carries off smoke. —*plural* **chim′ neys**

chop (chäp) *verb*   to cut with an ax or other sharp tool [The lumberjack *chopped* down a tree.] —**chopped, chop′ ping**

cit·y (sit′ ē) *noun*   a large town. —*plural* **cit′ ies**

clap (klap) *verb*   to hit the palms of the hands together [The audience *clapped* after the play.] —**clapped, clap′ ping**

class (klas) *noun*   a group of students meeting together to be taught [My English *class* is at 9 o'clock.] —*plural* **class′ es**

class·room (klas′ room) *noun*   a room in a school where classes meet to be taught. —*plural* **class′ rooms**

clean (klēn) *adjective*   without dirt [The room is *clean*.] —**clean′ er, clean′ est**   ♦*verb*   to remove dirt from [Please *clean* the oven.] —**cleaned, clean′ ing**

clear (klir) *adjective*   without clouds [Today was a *clear*, sunny day.] —**clear′ er, clear′ est**

cliff (klif) *noun*   a steep rock that goes almost straight down. —*plural* **cliffs**

climb (klīm) *verb*   to go up or down using feet or hands [We like to *climb* up trees.] —**climbed, climb′ ing**

clock (kläk) *noun*   a device for measuring and showing time. —*plural* **clocks**

close (klōz) *verb*   to shut [*Close* the door.] —**closed, clos′ ing**

clos·et (kläz′ it) *noun*   a small room or cupboard for clothes, linens, or supplies [The clothes were hung in the *closet*.] —*plural* **clos′ ets**

cloud (kloud) *noun*   many drops of water floating in the air. —*plural* **clouds**

coach (kōch) *noun*   a person who teaches and trains athletes or students. —*plural* **coach′ es**

coast (kōst) *noun*　land along the sea [The boat sailed toward the *coast*.] —*plural* **coasts**

coat (kōt) *noun*　an outer garment with sleeves. —*plural* **coats**

co·coa (kō′ kō) *noun*　a drink made from the powder of roasted cacao seeds.

colt (kōlt) *noun*　a young male horse or donkey [The *colt* stood by its mother.] —*plural* **colts**

comb (kōm) *noun*　a thin strip of hard material with teeth, used to arrange hair. ◆*verb*　to smooth or clean with a comb. —**combed, comb′ ing**

come (kum) *verb*　to move from there to here [Will you *come* to our party?] —**came, come, com′ ing**

com·pa·ny (kum′ pə nē) *noun*　**1** a group of people joined in some work [She works for a large *company*.] **2** guest or guests [We invited *company* for dinner.] —*plural* **com′ pa·nies**

com·pass (kum′ pəs) *noun*　an instrument for showing direction. —*plural* **com′ pass·es**

cop·i·er (käp′ ē ər) *noun*　a duplicating machine. —*plural* **cop′ i·ers**

cop·y (käp′ ē) *noun*　imitation [Make four *copies* of this letter.] —*plural* **cop′ ies** ◆*verb*　to make a copy or copies of [*Copy* the questions on the chalkboard.] —**cop′ ied, cop′ y·ing**

corn (kôrn) *noun*　a grain that grows in kernels on large ears.

cor·ner (kôr′ nər) *noun*　the place where two streets meet. —*plural* **cor′ ners**

cot·ton (kät′ 'n) *noun*　a type of cloth [This shirt is made of *cotton*.] —*plural* **cot′ tons**

couch (kouch) *noun*　furniture for sitting on; sofa. —*plural* **couch′ es**

could·n't (kood′ 'nt) could not.

count (kount) *verb*　to name numbers in order [Can you *count* to fifty?] —**count′ ed, count′ ing**

cous·in (kuz′ 'n) *noun*　the son or daughter of one's uncle or aunt. —*plural* **cous′ ins**

cow·boy (kou′ boi) *noun*　a ranch worker who herds cattle. —*plural* **cow′ boys**

crack·er (krak′ ər) *noun*　a thin, crisp biscuit. —*plural* **crack′ ers**

crash (krash) *verb*　to hit with great force [The bull *crashed* through the fence.] —**crashed, crash′ ing** ◆*noun*　the smashing of a car or airplane [They were hurt in a car *crash*.] —*plural* **crash′ es**

creek (krēk *or* krik) *noun*　a small stream [A *creek* wound through the meadow.] —*plural* **creeks**

crumb (krum) *noun*　a tiny piece broken off from bread or cake. —*plural* **crumbs**

crunch (krunch) *verb*　to chew with a noisy, crackling sound [*Crunch* the raw carrots.] —**crunch′ es, crunch′ ing**

crunch·y (krunch′ ē) *adjective*　making a crunching sound. —**crunch′ i·er, crunch′ i·est**

cry (krī) *verb*　to show feeling by shedding tears. —**cried, cry′ ing**

cud·dle (kud′ 'l) *verb*　to hold lovingly in one's arms [I like to *cuddle* the baby.] —**cud′ dled, cud′ dling**

a	fat	ir	here	ou	out	zh	leisure
ā	ape	ī	bite, fire	u	up	ng	ring
ä	car, lot	ō	go	ʉr	fur		a *in* ago
e	ten	ô	law, horn	ch	chin		e *in* agent
er	care	oi	oil	sh	she	ə =	i *in* unity
ē	even	oo	look	th	thin		o *in* collect
i	hit	o͞o	tool	*th*	then		u *in* focus

D

dai·sy (dā′ zē) *noun*   a common flower with white or pink petals around a yellow center. —*plural* **dai′ sies**

danc·er (dan′ sər) *noun*   a person who dances. —*plural* **danc′ ers**

dark (därk) *adjective*   having little or no light [This is a *dark* room.] —**dark′ er, dark′ est**

daugh·ter (dôt′ ər) *noun*   a girl or woman as she is related to a parent or to both parents. —*plural* **daugh′ ters**

day (dā) *noun*   a period of 24 hours, from midnight to midnight. —*plural* **days**

dear (dir) *adjective*   much loved [He visited his *dear* friend.] —**dear′ er, dear′ est**

de·cay (di kā′) *verb*   to become rotten by the action of bacteria [The fallen apples *decayed* on the ground.] —**de·cayed′, de·cay′ing**

deer (dir) *noun*   a swift-running, hoofed animal. —*plural* **deer**

de·lay (di lā′) *verb*   to put off to a later time [The freight train *delayed* traffic.] —**de·layed′, de·lay′ ing**

de·light·ed (di līt′ id) *adjective*   highly pleased.

de·ny (di nī′) *verb*   to say that something is not true [They *denied* breaking the window.] —**de·nied′, de·ny′ ing**

de·stroy (di stroi′) *verb*   to break up, tear down, or ruin [The flood *destroyed* 300 homes.] —**de·stroyed′, de·stroy′ ing**

did·n't (did′ ′nt) did not.

dig (dig) *verb*   to turn up ground. —**dug, dig′ ging**

din·ner (din′ ər) *noun*   the main meal of the day. —*plural* **din′ ners**

dip (dip) *verb*   to put into a liquid and quickly pull out again [*Dip* the brush into the paint.] —**dipped, dip′ ping**

dip·per (dip′ ər) *noun*   ladle. —*plural* **dip′ pers**

dish (dish) *noun*   any plate or bowl used to serve food. —*plural* **dish′ es**

doc·tor (däk′ tər) *noun*   a person trained to heal the sick. —*plural* **doc′ tors**

does·n't (duz′ ′nt) does not.

dol·lar (däl′ ər) *noun*   a U.S. coin or paper money. —*plural* **dol′ lars**

don·key (dang′ kē *or* dông′ kē) *noun*   an animal like a small horse with long ears. —*plural* **don′ keys**

don't (dōnt) do not.

door·knob (dôr′ näb′) *noun*   a small knob on a door, usually for releasing the latch.

doz·en (duz′ ′n) *noun*   a group of twelve [The carton holds a *dozen* eggs.] —*plural* **doz′ ens**

draw·er (drô′ ər) *noun*   a box that slides in and out of a table, chest, or desk. —*plural* **draw′ ers**

drear·y (drir′ ē) *adjective*   gloomy, sad, or dull [That's such a long, *dreary* tale.] —**drear′ i·er, drear′ i·est**

dress (dres) *noun*   the outer garment worn by girls and women. —*plural* **dress′ es**

dress·er (dres′ ər) *noun*   a chest of drawers for a bedroom [My clothes are folded in the *dresser*.] —*plural* **dress′ ers**

drib·ble (drib′ ′l) *verb*   to control a ball with short bounces or kicks. —**drib′ bled, drib′ bling**

drift (drift) *verb*   to be carried along by a current of water or air [The raft will *drift* downstream.] —**drift′ ed, drift′ ing**

drive (drīv) *verb*   to control a car, bus, or horse. —**drove, driv′ en, driv′ ing**

drop (dräp) *verb*   to fall or let fall [He *dropped* his lunch in the mud.] —**dropped, drop′ ping**

drop·per (dräp′ ər) *noun*   a small glass tube used to measure out a liquid in drops. —*plural* **drop′ pers**

drum (drum) *noun*   an instrument played by beating. —*plural* **drums**

drum·mer (drum′ ər) *noun*   a person who plays a drum. —*plural* **drum′ mers**

dry (drī) *verb*   to make or become dry. —**dried, dry′ ing**

dur·ing (door′ ing *or* dyoor′ ing) *preposition*   throughout the whole time of [Food was hard to get *during* the war.]

du·ty (doot′ ē) *noun*   any of the things that are supposed to be done. —*plural* **du′ ties**

E

early (ur′ lē) *adverb, adjective*   **1** near the beginning; soon after the start [in the *early* afternoon; *early* in his career].   **2** before the usual time [The bus came *early*.] —**ear′ li·er, ear′ li·est**

earn (urn) *verb*   to get pay for work done [She *earns* $5 an hour.] —**earned, earn′ ing**

earth (urth) *noun*   soil or ground [Farmers seed the *earth*.]

eas·y (ē′ zē) *adjective*   not hard to do or learn. —**eas′ i·er, eas′ i·est**

elf (elf) *noun*   a small fairy in folk tales. —*plural* **elves**

else (els) *adjective*   not the same; other [I thought you were someone *else*.]

em·ploy (im ploi′) *verb*   to hire and pay for the work of. —**em·ployed′, em·ploy′ ing**

en·e·my (en′ ə mē) *noun*   a person or group who hates or fights another. —*plural* **en′ e·mies**

en·joy (in joi′) *verb*   to get pleasure from [We *enjoyed* the ball game.] —**en·joyed′, en·joy′ ing**

e·qual (ē′ kwəl) *adjective*   of the same amount, size, or value.

e·rase (i rās′) *verb*   to rub out [I had to *erase* my mistake.] —**e·rased′, e·ras′ ing**

e·ras·er (i rā′ sər) *noun*   a thing that erases. —*plural* **e·ras′ ers**

er·rand (er′ ənd) *noun*   a short trip to do a thing. —*plural* **er′ rands**

e·ven (ē′ vən) *adjective*   flat, smooth [This is an *even* surface.]

eve·ning (ēv′ ning) *noun*   the close of day and early part of night [The *evening* shadows lengthen as the sun sets.] —*plural* **eve′ nings**

ev·er·y (ev′ rē) *adjective*   each [He knows *every* person here.]

ex·plode (ik splōd′) *verb*   to blow up with a loud noise [The firecracker *exploded*.] —**ex·plod′ ed, ex·plod′ ing**

F

fall (fôl) *verb*   to come down suddenly; tumble. —**fell, fall′ en, fall′ ing**

fam·i·ly (fam′ ə lē) *noun*   a group made up of parents and their children. —*plural* **fam′ i·lies**

fas·ten (fas′ ’n) *verb*   attach [The collar is *fastened* to the shirt.] —**fas′ ten, fas′ ten·ing**

fa·ther (fä′ thər) *noun*   a male parent. —*plural* **fa′ thers**

fear (fir) *noun*   the feeling of being near to danger or pain [I have a *fear* of large, barking dogs.] —*plural* **fears**

feed (fēd) *verb*   to give food to. —**fed, feed′ ing**

fer·ry (fer′ ē) *noun*   a boat used to take people and cars across a river. —*plural* **fer′ ries**

a	fat	ir	here	ou	out	zh	leisure	
ā	ape	ī	bite, fire	u	up	ng	ring	
ä	car, lot	ō	go	ur	fur			a *in* ago
e	ten	ô	law, horn	ch	chin			e *in* agent
er	care	oi	oil	sh	she	ə	=	i *in* unity
ē	even	oo	look	th	thin			o *in* collect
i	hit	oo	tool	th	then			u *in* focus

fid·dle (fid′ 'l) *noun* a violin. —*plural*
fid′ dles

fight (fīt) *verb* battle; struggle [The children
began to *fight*.] —**fought, fight′ ing**

find (fīnd) *verb* to get back something that has
been lost [We *found* the missing book.]
—**found, find′ ing**

fin·ger (fing′ gər) *noun* any of the five parts at
the end of the hand. —*plural* **fin′ gers**

fire (fīr) *noun* the heat and light of something
burning. —*plural* **fires**

fix (fiks) *verb* to make stay in place. —**fixed,
fix′ ing**

flag (flag) *noun* a piece of cloth with colors and
designs used as a symbol of a country or state.
—*plural* **flags**

flash·light (flash′ līt) *noun* a battery-operated
light that is carried. —*plural* **flash′ lights**

flat (flat) *adjective* smooth and level.
—**flat′ ter, flat′ test**

fli·er (flī′ ər) *noun* a person who flies an
airplane. —*plural* **fli′ ers**

flight (flīt) *noun* a trip through the air [We made
a 500-mile *flight*.] —*plural* **flights**

float (flōt) *verb* to rest on top of water [The raft
floated on the lake.] —**float′ ed, float′ ing**

flood (flud) *noun* an overflowing of water on
land [Heavy rains caused a *flood*.] —*plural*
floods

flour (flour) *noun* grain that has been ground
into a fine powder.

fly (flī) *verb* to move through the air [Birds *fly*
south each winter.] —**flew, flown, fly′ ing**
◆*noun* a flying insect [Swat that *fly*!] —*plural*
flies

fog·gy (fôg′ ē *or* fäg′ ē) *adjective* covered with
fog [It was too *foggy* to see.] —**fog′ gi·er,
fog′ gi·est**

fol·low (fäl′ ō) *verb* to go after [The dog
followed him home.] —**fol′ lowed, fol′ low·ing**

foot (foot) *noun* the end of the leg, on which
one stands or moves. —*plural* **feet**

fore·cast (fôr′ kast) *verb* to tell how something
will turn out; predict [Rain is *forecast* for
tomorrow.] —**fore′ cast** *or* **fore′ cast·ed,
fore′ cast·ing**

for·get (fər get′) *verb* to be unable to remember
[I *forgot* her address.] —**for·got′, for·got′ ten,
for·get′ ting**

fork (fôrk) *noun* a tool with prongs at one end
used to pick up something. —*plural* **forks**

forth (fôrth) *adverb* forward or onward.

foun·tain (foun′ t'n) *noun* a thing built for a
stream of water to rise and fall in [Get a drink at
the *fountain*.] —*plural* **foun′ tains**

fox (fäks) *noun* a small animal with pointed
ears, bushy tail, and reddish fur. —*plural*
fox′ es

freeze (frēz) *verb* to harden into ice. —**froze,
fro′ zen, freez′ ing**

friend (frend) *noun* a person whom one knows
well and likes. —*plural* **friends**

fright·en (frīt′ 'n) *verb* to scare.
—**fright′ ened, fright′ en·ing**

from (frum *or* främ) *preposition* starting at;
out of.

fry (frī) *verb* to cook in hot fat [We *fried*
chicken for dinner.] —**fried, fry′ ing**

full (fool) *adjective* filled [This is a *full* jar.]

fun·ny (fun′ ē) *adjective* causing smiles or
laughter. —**fun′ ni·er, fun′ ni·est**

fur (fʉr) *noun* the soft, thick hair that covers
many animals. —*plural* **furs**

fur·ry (fʉr′ ē) *adjective* covered with fur.
—**fur′ ri·er, fur′ ri·est**

G

gain (gān) *verb*   to increase [He *gained* ten pounds in two months.] —**gained, gain′ ing**

gal·lon (gal′ ən) *noun*   a measure of liquids equal to four quarts. —*plural* **gal′ lons**

gas (gas) *noun*   something that has the same form as the air [Oxygen is a *gas*.] —*plural* **gas′ es**

gear (gir) *noun*   part of an arrangement of notched wheels within a machine that pass motion to each other [The *gears* of the car were rusty.] —*plural* **gears**

gig·gle (gig′ ′l) *verb*   to laugh in a silly way. —**gig′ gled, gig′ gling**

girl (gʉrl) *noun*   a female child. —*plural* **girls**

glass (glas) *noun*   **1** a hard substance that lets light through [The windows are made of *glass*.] **2** a container for drinking [Pour milk into my *glass*.] —*plural* **glass′ es**

glove (gluv) *noun*   a covering to protect the hand [Surgeons wear rubber *gloves*.] —*plural* **gloves**

glue (glo͞o) *noun*   a sticky substance ♦*verb*   to stick together with glue [She *glued* the broken plate together.] —**glued, glu′ ing**

go (gō) *verb*   to move away; leave. —**went, go′ ing**

goat (gōt) *noun*   a cud-chewing animal with horns. —*plural* **goats**

gold·fish (gōld′ fish) *noun*   a small, orange fish kept in ponds or fishbowls. —*plural* **gold′ fish**

gone (gôn) *a past form of* **go**   moved away; departed.

goose (go͞os) *noun*   a swimming bird like a duck but with a longer neck. —*plural* **geese**

grand·fa·ther (gran′ fä′ *th*ər *or* grand′ fä′ *th*ər) *noun*   the father of one's father or mother. —*plural* **grand′ fa·thers**

grand·moth·er (gran′ mu*th*′ ər *or* grand′ mu*th*′ ər) *noun*   the mother of one's father or mother. —*plural* **grand′ moth′ ers**

grape (grāp) *noun*   a small fruit with a smooth skin. —*plural* **grapes**

grease (grēs) *noun*   any soft, oily substance.

greas·y (grē′sē *or* grē′ zē) *adjective*   smeared with grease [Look at those *greasy* hands!] —**greas′ i·er, greas′ i·est**

grim·y (grī′ mē) *adjective*   very dirty. —**grim′ i·er, grim′ i·est**

grin (grin) *verb*   to make a big or foolish smile [The clown *grinned* at us.] —**grinned, grin′ ning**

groan (grōn) *verb*   to make a sound showing sadness or pain [We *groaned* when our team lost.] —**groaned, groan′ ing**

ground (ground) *noun*   land; earth.

guess (ges) *verb*   to judge or decide about something without knowing for certain [Can you *guess* how old he is?] —**guessed, guess′ ing**

H

had·n't (had′ ′nt)   had not.

hair (her) *noun*   growth that comes from the skin of human beings and some animals [I must comb my *hair*.]

half (haf) *noun*   either of the two equal parts of something [Five is *half* of ten.] —*plural* **halves**

ham·burg·er (ham′ bʉr′ gər) *noun*   a small, flat patty of ground beef. —*plural* **ham′ burg·ers**

a	fat	ir	here	ou	out	zh	leisure
ā	ape	ī	bite, fire	u	up	ng	ring
ä	car, lot	ō	go	ʉr	fur		a *in* ago
e	ten	ô	law, horn	ch	chin		e *in* agent
er	care	oi	oil	sh	she	ə =	i *in* unity
ē	even	o͞o	look	th	thin		o *in* collect
i	hit	o͞o	tool	*th*	then		u *in* focus

hap·pen (hap′ ′n) *verb* to take place, especially by chance [What *happened* at school today?] —**hap′ pened, hap′ pen·ing**

hap·py (hap′ ē) *adjective* feeling joy and gladness. —**hap′ pi·er, hap′ pi·est**

har·bor (här′ bər) *noun* a port. —*plural* **har′ bors**

has·n't (haz′ ′nt) has not.

haste (hāst) *noun* a hurrying in a careless way [*Haste* makes waste.]

hast·y (hās′ tē) *adjective* done or made too quickly [Don't make a *hasty* decision.] —**hast′ i·er, hast′ i·est**

have (hav) *verb* to be the owner of [She *has* a car.] —**had, hav′ ing**

health·y (hel′ thē) *adjective* well [She is a *healthy* child.] —**health′ i·er, health′ i·est**

hear (hir) *verb* to receive sound through the ears [I *hear* music.] —**heard, hear′ ing**

heart (härt) *noun* the muscle in the body that moves blood. —*plural* **hearts**

heav·y (hev′ ē) *adjective* weighing very much [The dog was too *heavy* to carry.] —**heav′ i·er, heav′ i·est**

height (hīt) *noun* the highest point or degree [The actor reached the *height* of fame.] —*plural* **heights**

he'll (hēl) he will.

herd (hurd) *noun* a number of cattle living together [They had a *herd* of 100 cows.] —*plural* **herds**

high (hī) *adjective* tall [That's a very *high* mountain.] —**high′ er, high′ est**

hike (hīk) *verb* to take a long walk in the woods or country [We *hiked* to the river.] —**hiked, hik′ ing**

hire (hīr) *verb* to employ [She has *hired* a new secretary.] —**hired, hir′ ing**

hog (hôg *or* häg) *noun* a pig, especially a full-grown pig raised for meat. —*plural* **hogs**

hold (hōld) *verb* to take and keep in the hands or arms [Please *hold* the baby for a while.] —**held, hold′ ing**

hol·i·day (höl′ ə dā) *noun* a day set aside to celebrate some event. —*plural* **hol′ i·days**

hon·ey (hun′ ē) *noun* a thick, sweet, yellow syrup made by bees [Mother spread *honey* on her roll.]

hop (häp) *verb* to leap on one foot. —**hopped, hop′ ping**

horn (hôrn) *noun* **1** a hard, pointed growth on the head of some animals. **2** a brass-wind instrument. —*plural* **horns**

hose (hōz) *noun* a tube through which fluid is sent [Use the garden *hose*.] —*plural* **hos′ es**

hot (hät) *adjective* having a high temperature. —**hot′ ter, hot′ test**

hour (our) *noun* 60 minutes. —*plural* **hours**

house (hous) *noun* a building for people to live in. —*plural* **hous′ es**

how's (houz) how is.

hud·dle (hud′ ′l) *noun* a huddling together of a football team to get signals for the next play. —*plural* **hud′ dles**

hun·gry (hung′ grē) *adjective* needing food. —**hun′ gri·er, hun′ gri·est**

hur·ry (hur′ ē) *verb* to move too quickly [We *hurried* because we were late.] —**hur′ ried, hur′ ry·ing**

hurt (hurt) *verb* to have pain [My head *hurts*.] —**hurt, hurt′ ing**

---

i·cy (ī′ sē) *adjective* slippery or very cold [He slipped on the *icy* steps.] —**i′ ci·er, i′ ci·est**

I'd (īd) **1** I had. **2** I would. **3** I should.

inch (inch) *noun* a unit of measure. —*plural* **inch′ es**

in·side (in′ sīd′) *noun* the part within [Wash the windows on the *inside*.]

in·vite (in vīt′) *verb* to ask to be one's guest [I *invited* her to dinner.] —**in·vit′ ed, in·vit′ ing**

I've (īv) I have.

J

jack·et (jak′ it) *noun* a short coat. —*plural* **jack′ ets**

jour·ney (jur′ nē) *noun* a trip [She took a *journey* around the world.] —*plural* **jour′neys**

jug·gle (jug′ ′l) *verb* to do tricks with the hands [He can *juggle* three balls at once.] —**jug′ gled, jug′ gling**

K

keep (kēp) *verb* **1** to have and not let go [*Keep* the change.] **2** to make last or continue [*Keep* your engine running.] —**kept, keep′ ing**

ket·tle (ket′ ′l) *noun* a teakettle. —*plural* **ket′ tles**

key (kē) *noun* a small metal device that locks or unlocks a door or drawer. —*plural* **keys**

knap·sack (nap′ sak) *noun* a bag worn on the back for carrying supplies. —*plural* **knap′ sacks**

knee (nē) *noun* the joint between the thigh and lower leg. —*plural* **knees**

kneel (nēl) *verb* to rest on a knee or knees [*Kneel* down to tie your shoes.] —**knelt, kneel′ ing**

knife (nīf) *noun* a cutting tool with a flat, sharp blade. —*plural* **knives**

knot (nät) *verb* to tie or fasten with a knot. —**knot′ ted, knot′ ting**

know (nō) *verb* to be aware of; realize [Does he *know* what happened?] —**knew, known, know′ ing**

knuck·le (nuk′ ′l) *noun* a joint of the finger. —*plural* **knuck′ les**

L

lad·der (lad′ ər) *noun* a frame of two long pieces connected by rungs, used for climbing. —*plural* **lad′ ders**

la·dy (lā′ dē) *noun* a woman. —*plural* **la′ dies**

lake (lāk) *noun* a large body of water surrounded by land. —*plural* **lakes**

a fat	**ir** here	**ou** out	**zh** leisure
ā ape	**ī** bite, fire	**u** up	**ng** ring
ä car, lot	**ō** go	**ʉr** fur	a *in* ago
e ten	**ô** law, horn	**ch** chin	e *in* agent
er care	**oi** oil	**sh** she	**ə** = i *in* unity
ē even	**oo** look	**th** thin	o *in* collect
i hit	**o̅o̅** tool	***th*** then	u *in* focus

lamb (lam) *noun*　a young sheep. —*plural* **lambs**

large (lärj) *adjective*　big [I have a *large* house.] —**larg′ er, larg′ est**

lat·er (lāt′ ər) *adverb*　after some time [Don't wait; I'll come *later*.]

lay (lā) *verb*　to put down to rest on or in something [*Lay* your books on the shelf.] —**laid, lay′ ing**

la·zy (lā′ zē) *adjective*　not willing to work hard [The *lazy* horse wouldn't move.] —**la′ zi·er, la′ zi·est**

lead·er (lē′ dər) *noun*　a person who leads or guides [Our scout *leader* likes hiking.] —*plural* **lead′ ers**

leaf (lēf) *noun*　a flat green part growing from the stem of a plant or tree. —*plural* **leaves**

learn (lʉrn) *verb*　to get some knowledge or skill [I have *learned* to knit.] —**learned, learn′ ing**

leave (lēv) *verb*　**1** to go away from [When did they *leave* the party?] **2** to let stay [*Leave* the door open.] —**left, leav′ ing**

leg (leg) *noun*　part of the body used for standing and walking. —*plural* **legs**

lem·on·ade (lem ə nād′) *noun*　a drink made of lemon juice, sugar, and water.

les·son (les′ 'n) *noun*　something to be learned by a student [She studied her math *lesson*.] —*plural* **les′ sons**

let's (lets) let us.

life (līf) *noun*　the time that a person or thing is alive [Her *life* has just begun.] —*plural* **lives**

light (līt) *noun*　**1** brightness [Is there enough *light* in this room?] **2** something that gives light, as a lamp [The room looked cheerful with the *light* on.] —*plural* **lights**

light·ning (līt′ ning) *noun*　a flash of light in the sky.

limb (lim) *noun*　**1** an arm, leg, or wing. **2** a large branch of a tree. —*plural* **limbs**

lit·tle (lit′ 'l) *adjective*　small in size [We live in a *little* house.] —**lit′ tler, lit′ tlest**

live (liv) *verb*　to make one's home [We *live* on a farm.] —**lived, liv′ ing**

load (lōd) *noun*　something that is carried at one time [He carried the heavy *load*.] —*plural* **loads**

loaf (lōf) *noun*　bread baked in one piece. —*plural* **loaves**

loan (lōn) *verb*　to lend something to be returned [I *loaned* him a dime.] —**loaned, loan′ ing**

log (lôg) *noun*　a part of a tree that has been cut down [We cut up *logs* for the fire.] —*plural* **logs**

loud (loud) *adjective*　strong in sound [Can you hear that *loud* noise?] —**loud′ er, loud′ est**

luck·y (luk′ ē) *adjective*　having good luck [She was *lucky* to win the contest.] —**luck′ i·er, luck′ i·est**

lunch (lunch) *noun*　the meal eaten between breakfast and dinner. —*plural* **lunch′ es**

M

man (man) *noun*　an adult male human being. —*plural* **men**

mar·ry (mar′ ē) *verb*　to take someone as husband or wife. —**mar′ ried, mar′ ry·ing**

may·be (mā′ bē) *adverb* perhaps.

melt (melt) *verb* to change from a solid to a liquid, as by heat [The sun *melted* the snow.] —**melt′ ed, melt′ ing**

mid·dle (mid′ ′l) *noun* the point that is halfway between the ends or in the center [The island is in the *middle* of the lake.]

mid·night (mid′ nīt) *noun* twelve o'clock at night.

might (mīt) *noun* great strength or power [Pull with all your *might*.]

mile (mīl) *noun* a measure of length equal to 5,280 feet. —*plural* **miles**

milk (milk) *noun* a white liquid used for drinking [I poured *milk* on my cereal.]

mil·lion (mil′ yən) *noun, adjective* a thousand thousands. —*plural* **mil′ lions**

mind (mīnd) *noun* intellect [The *mind* was once thought of as apart from the body.] —*plural* **minds**

min·ute (min′ it) *noun* a period of time; 60 seconds [Turn off the oven in ten *minutes*.] —*plural* **min′ utes**

mon·key (mung′ kē) *noun* any animal of the group that appears most like man. —*plural* **mon′ keys**

month (munth) *noun* any of the twelve parts into which the year is divided [Thanksgiving comes in the *month* of November.] —*plural* **months**

more (môr) *adjective* greater in amount or degree [He has *more* free time than I do.]

morn·ing (môr′ ning) *noun* the early part of the day [Joe slept late this *morning*.]

moss (môs) *noun* tiny green plants growing in clumps like velvet [*Moss* covered the rock.]

moth·er (mu*th*′ ər) *noun* a female parent —*plural* **moth′ ers**

moun·tain (moun′ t'n) *noun* a very high hill [We climbed a steep *mountain*.] —*plural* **moun′ tains**

mouse (mous) *noun* a small, gnawing animal. —*plural* **mice**

mouth (mouth) *noun* the opening in the head for eating and making sounds [The soup burned my *mouth*.] —*plural* **mouths**

move (mo͞ov) *verb* **1** to change place or position [*Move* the picture to the left.] **2** to change the place where one lives [They *moved* to New York.] —**moved, mov′ ing**

mud·dy (mud′ ē) *adjective* full of mud [Clean your *muddy* boots.] —**mud′ di·er, mud′ di·est**

mul·ti·ply (mul′ tə plī) *verb* to repeat a figure a certain number of times [She *multiplied* 3 by 4 to get 12.] —**mul′ ti·plied, mul′ ti·ply·ing**

N

nap·kin (nap′ kin) *noun* a piece of cloth or paper used while eating to protect clothes or to wipe fingers or lips. —*plural* **nap′ kins**

near (nir) *adjective* not far; close [Our house is *near* to the school.] —**near′ er, near′ est**

neigh·bor (nā′ bər) *noun* a person who lives near another. —*plural* **neigh′ bors**

a	fat	ir	here	ou	out	zh	leisure
ā	ape	ī	bite, fire	u	up	ng	ring
ä	car, lot	ō	go	ʉr	fur		a *in* ago
e	ten	ô	law, horn	ch	chin		e *in* agent
er	care	oi	oil	sh	she	ə =	i *in* unity
ē	even	o͞o	look	th	thin		o *in* collect
i	hit	o͞o	tool	*th*	then		u *in* focus

neph·ew (nef′ yoo) *noun* the son of one's brother or sister. —*plural* **neph′ ews**

nev·er (nev′ ər) *adverb* not ever [I *never* saw her again.]

new (noo) *adjective* that has not been worn or used [We sell *new* and used cars.] —**new′ er, new′ est**

news·pa·per (nooz′ pā′ pər) *noun* publication containing news, ideas, and advertisements. —*plural* **news′ pa′ pers**

nib·ble (nib′ ′l) *noun* a small bite. —*plural* **nib′ bles**

niece (nēs) *noun* the daughter of one's brother or sister. —*plural* **niec′ es**

night (nīt) *noun* the time of darkness between sunset and sunrise. —*plural* **nights**

noise (noiz) *noun* a loud, harsh sound [Listen to the *noise* of the fireworks.] —*plural* **nois′ es**

nois·y (noi′ zē) *adjective* making noise [The class is too *noisy*.] —**nois′ i·er, nois′ i·est**

none (nun) *pronoun* no one. [*None* of us is ready.]

north (nôrth) *noun* the direction to the right of a person facing the sunset.

numb (num) *adjective* not able to feel [My toes were *numb* with cold.] —**numb′ er, numb′ est**

num·ber (num′ bər) *noun* a symbol or word used in counting or that tells how many [Two, 7, and tenth are all *numbers*.] —*plural* **num′ bers**

nurse (nurs) *noun* a person trained to care for sick people. —*plural* **nurs′ es**

O

oak (ōk) *noun* a large tree with hard wood and nuts called acorns. —*plural* **oaks**

oat (ōt) *noun* a cereal grass whose grain is used as food. —*plural* **oats**

o·bey (ō bā′) *verb* to carry out the orders of [Our dog *obeys* our commands.] —**o·beyed′, o·bey′ ing**

once (wuns) *adverb* one time. [We eat together *once* a week.]

o·pen (ō′ p′n) *verb* to make or become open [Please *open* that trunk.] —**o′ pened, o′ pen·ing**

or·der (ôr′ dər) *noun* a direction telling someone what to do [The general gave his troops an *order*.] ◆*verb* to tell someone what to do [The police officer *ordered* the crowd to move.] —**or′ dered, or′ der·ing**

out (out) *adverb* away from the inside or center [Come *out* and play.]

out·doors (out′ dôrz′) *adverb* in the open; outside [We ran *outdoors* to play.]

out·fit (out′ fit) *noun* clothing used in some activity [Wear a hiking *outfit*.] —*plural* **out′ fits**

out·side (out′ sīd′) *adverb* on or to the outside [Let's play *outside*.]

o·ver (ō′ vər) *preposition* in, at, or to a place above [Hang the picture *over* the fireplace.]

o·ver·sleep (ō vər slēp′) *verb* to sleep past the time one meant to get up [Lisa *overslept* today.] —**o·ver·slept′, o·ver·sleep′ ing**

ox (äks) *noun* a male of the cattle family. —*plural* **oxen**

P

pail (pāl) *noun* a round, deep container for holding and carrying liquids. —*plural* **pails**

paint·er (pānt′ ər) *noun* an artist who paints pictures. —*plural* **paint′ ers**

pair (per) *noun*　a set of two [I have a new *pair* of skates.]

pa·per (pā′ pər) *noun*　a thin material used to write on. —*plural* **pa′ pers**

par·ty (pär′ tē) *noun*　a gathering of people to have fun. —*plural* **par′ ties**

pass (pas) *verb*　to go by [I *passed* your house today.] —**passed, pass′ ing**

paste (pāst) *noun*　a mixture used for sticking paper or other things together. ◆*verb*　to make stick [Let's *paste* pictures in this book.] —**past′ ed, past′ ing**

pear (per) *noun*　a soft, yellow or green juicy fruit. —*plural* **pears**

pearl (purl) *noun*　a hard, round stone formed inside oysters and often used in jewelry. —*plural* **pearls**

pen·ny (pen′ ē) *noun*　a cent. —*plural* **pen′ nies**

pep·per (pep′ ər) *noun*　a hot-tasting seasoning.

per·haps (pər haps′) *adverb*　possibly; maybe [*Perhaps* it will rain.]

per·son (pur′ s'n) *noun*　a human being [I know every *person* in this room.] —*plural* **per′ sons**

pic·nic (pik′ nik) *noun*　a meal eaten outdoors [We will have our *picnic* in the park.] —*plural* **pic′ nics**

pic·ture (pik′ chər) *noun*　a drawing, painting, or photograph. —*plural* **pic′ tures**

pile (pīl) *noun*　a mass of things heaped together [We made a big *pile* of leaves.] —*plural* **piles**

pin (pin) *noun*　a thin, sharp wire used to fasten things. ◆*verb*　to fasten with a pin [He *pinned* the badge to his sweater.] —**pinned, pin′ ning**

pint (pīnt) *noun*　a measure of volume equal to ½ quart. —*plural* **pints**

pitch·er (pich′ ər) *noun*　the baseball player who pitches the balls to the batters. —*plural* **pitch′ ers**

place (plās) *noun*　a city, town, or village. —*plural* **plac′ es**

plan (plan) *verb*　to think of a way of making or doing something [We *planned* our party.] —**planned, plan′ ning**

plant (plant) *noun*　a living thing that makes its own food [Many *plants* were growing in the garden.] ◆*verb*　to put into the ground to grow [We *planted* corn in our yard.] —**plant′ ed, plant′ ing**

play (plā) *verb*　to have fun [Children like to *play* outdoors.] —**played, play′ ing** ◆*noun*　a story acted out on stage, radio, or television [They went to see a *play*.] —*plural* **plays**

play·ground (plā′ ground) *noun*　a place for outdoor games and play. —*plural* **play′ grounds**

plumb·er (plum′ ər) *noun*　a person who repairs water and gas pipes. —*plural* **plumb′ ers**

po·ny (pō′ nē) *noun*　a type of small horse. —*plural* **po′ nies**

pour (pôr) *verb*　to let flow in a steady stream [The milk was *poured* into glasses.] —**poured, pour′ ing**

praise (prāz) *verb*　to say good things about [My teacher *praised* my work.] —**praised, prais′ ing**

press (pres) *verb*　to put steady weight on [He *pressed* the doorbell.] —**pressed, press′ ing**

pret·ty (prit′ ē *or* pur′ tē) *adjective*　nice to look at or hear. —**pret′ ti·er, pret′ ti·est**

price (prīs) *noun*　the cost of something. —*plural* **pric′ es**

prin·cess (prin′ sis) *noun*　daughter of a king or queen. —*plural* **prin′ ces·ses**

a	fat	ir	here	ou	out	zh	leisure
ā	ape	ī	bite, fire	u	up	ng	ring
ä	car, lot	ō	go	ur	fur		a *in* ago
e	ten	ô	law, horn	ch	chin		e *in* agent
er	care	oi	oil	sh	she	ə =	i *in* unity
ē	even	oo	look	th	thin		o *in* collect
i	hit	oo	tool	th	then		u *in* focus

prize (prīz) *noun* something given to a winner of a contest [The *prize* is a blue ribbon.] —*plural* **priz′ es**

prog·ress (präg′ res) *noun* a developing or improving [She shows *progress* in learning French.] ♦*verb* (prə gres′) to move forward. —**pro·gressed′, pro·gress′ ing**

pry (prī) *verb* to raise or move with a lever or crowbar. —**pried, pry′ ing**

pud·dle (pud′ ′l) *noun* a small pool of water [Stay out of the *puddles* after the rain.] —*plural* **pud′ dles**

pull (pool) *verb* to move or draw closer [*Pull* up your socks.] —**pulled, pull′ ing**

pump·kin (pum′ kin *or* pung′ kin) *noun* a large, round, orange fruit that grows on a vine. —*plural* **pump′ kins**

pup·py (pup′ ē) *noun* a young dog. —*plural* **pup′ pies**

puz·zle (puz′ ′l) *noun* a toy or problem that tests one's cleverness or skill [Let's put the jigsaw *puzzle* together.] —*plural* **puz′ zles**

R

race (rās) *noun* a contest of speed [Her horse won the *race*.] —*plural* **rac′ es** ♦ *verb* to have a race with [I'll *race* you to the corner.] —**raced, rac′ ing**

rad·ish (rad′ ish) *noun* a sharp-tasting root which is eaten raw. —*plural* **rad′ ish·es**

rain (rān) *noun* water that falls to the earth in drops. ♦*verb* to fall as rain [It is *raining*.] —**rained, rain′ ing**

rain·coat (rān′ kōt) *noun* a waterproof coat. —*plural* **rain′ coats**

rain·y (rā′ nē) *adjective* having much rain [Ball games are cancelled on *rainy* days.] —**rain′ i·er, rain′ i·est**

ranch (ranch) *noun* a large farm for raising cattle, horses, or sheep. —*plural* **ranch′ es**

rat·tle (rat′ ′l) *noun* a baby's toy that rattles when shaken. —*plural* **rat′ tles**

ray (rā) *noun* a narrow beam of light [The *rays* of the flashlight are bright.] —*plural* **rays**

rear (rir) *adjective* at or in the back part [Please deliver groceries to the *rear* door.]

re·bound (ri bound′) *verb* to bounce back [Aaron caught the ball as it *rebounded* from the fence.] —**re·bound′ ed, re·bound′ ing** ♦ (rē′ bound) **1** a bouncing or bounding back. **2** an object that bounces back.

re·build (rē bild′) *verb* to build again. —**re·built′, re·build′ ing**

rec·ord (rek′ ərd) *noun* a disc on which sound has been recorded. —*plural* **rec′ ords**

re·fill (rē fil′) *verb* to fill again. —**re·filled′, re·fill′ ing**

re·gain (ri gān′) *verb* to get back again [He *regained* his health slowly.] —**re·gained′, re·gain′ ing**

re·hearse (ri hʉrs′) *verb* to practice a play or speech. —**re·hearsed′, re·hears′ ing**

re·heat (rē hēt′) *verb* to make warm again [The cook will *reheat* the soup.] —**re·heat′ ed, re·heat′ ing**

re·mind (ri mīnd′) *verb* to make remember [*Remind* me to pay the gas bill.] —**re·mind′ ed, re·mind′ ing**

re·new (ri noo′) *verb* to make new or fresh again [*Renew* that old table by painting it.] —**re·newed′, re·new′ ing**

re·paint (rē pānt′) *verb* to paint again. —**re·paint′ ed, re·paint′ ing**

re·pay (ri pā′) *verb* to pay back [Always *repay* a loan.] —**re·paid′, re·pay′ ing**

re·place (ri plās′) *verb* to put another in the place of something used, lost, or broken [*Replace* the worn tire.] —**re·placed′, re·plac′ ing**

re·ply (ri plī′) *verb* to answer [*Reply* to my question.] —**re·plied′, re·ply′ ing**

re·print (rē print′) *verb* to publish again. —**re·print′ ed, re·print′ ing**

re·read (rē rēd′) *verb* to read again. —**re·read′, re·read′ ing**

re·take (rē tāk′) *verb* to take again or take back. —**re·took′, re·tak′ en, re·tak′ ing**

re·teach (rē tēch′) *verb* to teach again. —**re·taught′, re·teach′ ing**

re·tell (rē tel′) *verb* to report or tell a story again. —**re·told′, re·tell′ ing**

re·think (rē think′) *verb* to think over again [We had better *rethink* our plans.] —**re·thought′, re·think′ ing**

re·turn (ri turn′) *verb* to go or send back [I will *return* this sweater.] —**re·turned′, re·turn′ ing**

re·view (ri vyoo′) *verb* to go over or study again [I have to *review* for the math test.] —**re·viewed′, re·view′ ing**

re·vis·it (rē viz′ it) *verb* to visit again. —**re·vis′ it·ed, re·vis′ it·ing**

re·wind (rē wind′) *verb* to wind again [Please *rewind* the hose.] —**re·wound′, re·wind′ ing**

re·write (rē rīt′) *verb* to write again or in different words [An author may *rewrite* a story several times.] —**re·wrote′, re·writ′ ing**

rib·bon (rib′ ən) *noun* a narrow strip used for tying or decorating things [He tied a red *ribbon* on the gift.] —*plural* **rib′ bons**

rid·dle (rid′ ′l) *noun* a puzzle with a tricky meaning or an answer that is hard to guess. —*plural* **rid′ dles**

ride (rīd) *verb* to sit on and make move [I like to *ride* horses.] —**rode, rid′ den, rid′ ing**

right (rīt) *adjective* **1** correct or true [That is the *right* way to go.] **2** opposite of left [Raise your *right* hand.]

ripe (rīp) *adjective* ready to be gathered and used for food. —**rip′ er, rip′ est**

rise (rīz) *verb* to move toward a higher place [The sun is *rising*.] —**rose, ris′ en, ris′ ing**

riv·er (riv′ ər) *noun* a large stream of water [The *river* flowed into the ocean.] —*plural* **riv′ ers**

road (rōd) *noun* highway. —*plural* **roads**

road·way (rōd′ wā) *noun* the part of the road on which cars and trucks travel [The truck blocked the *roadway*.] —*plural* **road′ ways**

roast (rōst) *verb* to cook in an oven or over a fire [We *roasted* a turkey.] —**roast′ ed, roast′ ing**

roll (rōl) *verb* to move by turning over and over [The dog *rolled* on the grass.] —**rolled, roll′ ing** ♦*noun* bread baked in a small, shaped piece. —*plural* **rolls**

roost·er (roos′ tər) a male chicken. [The *rooster* crowed at dawn.] —*plural* **roost′ ers**

round (round) *adjective* shaped like a ball or circle [The earth is *round*.]

run·way (run′ wā) *noun* a long strip of land on which airplanes take off and land. —*plural* **run′ ways**

S

sad (sad) *adjective* causing an unhappy feeling [They cried at the *sad* news.] —**sad′ der, sad′ dest**

a	fat	ir	here	ou	out	zh	leisure
ā	ape	ī	bite, fire	u	up	ng	ring
ä	car, lot	ō	go	ur	fur		a *in* ago
e	ten	ô	law, horn	ch	chin		e *in* agent
er	care	oi	oil	sh	she	ə =	i *in* unity
ē	even	oo	look	th	thin		o *in* collect
i	hit	oo	tool	*th*	then		u *in* focus

sad·dle (sad′ ′l) *noun*   a seat for a rider on a horse. —*plural* **sad′ dles**

salt·y (sôl′ tē) *adjective*   tasting of salt [Pretzels are *salty*.] —**salt′ i·er, salt′ i·est**

sand·y (san′ dē) *adjective*   full of sand [That is a *sandy* shore.] —**sand′ i·er, sand′ i·est**

save (sāv) *verb*   **1** to rescue [He was *saved* from drowning.] **2** to keep or store up [She *saves* bottle caps.] —**saved, sav′ ing**

say (sā) *verb*   to speak [Can this parrot *say* its name?] —**said, say′ ing**

scis·sors (siz′ ərz) *noun plural*   a two-bladed tool used for cutting.

scout (skout) *verb*   to look for something [The campers *scouted* for firewood.] —**scout′ed, scout′ ing**

scrape (skrāp) *verb*   to rub the surface or skin from [He fell and *scraped* his knee.] —**scraped, scrap′ ing**

scrib·ble (skrib′ ′l) *verb*   to write quickly or carelessly. —**scrib′ bled, scrib′ bling**

scur·ry (skur′ ē) *verb*   to run quickly; scamper. —**scur′ ried, scur′ ry·ing**

search (surch) *verb*   to look in order to find something [We *searched* the house.] —**searched, search′ ing**

see (sē) *verb*   to look; to use one's sight [I need glasses to *see* well.] —**saw, seen, see′ ing**

send (send) *verb*   to cause to go or be carried [*Send* them home for their lunch.] —**sent, send′ ing**

set·tle (set′ ′l) *verb* to come to an agreement or decision [We *settled* our argument.] —**set′ tled, set′ tling**

shad·y (shād′ ē) *adjective*   shaded from the sun [It was *shady* in the forest.] —**shad′ i·er, shad′ i·est**

shall (shal) *helping verb*   [I *shall* leave tomorrow.]

share (sher) *verb*   to divide and give out [She *shared* her candy with us.] —**shared, shar′ ing**

she'd (shēd)   **1** she had.   **2** she would.

sheep (shēp) *noun*   a cud-chewing animal that is covered with wool. —*plural* **sheep**

shelf (shelf) *noun*   a thin, flat length of wood or metal used to hold things [Put the book on the top *shelf*.] —*plural* **shelves**

shell (shel) *noun*   a hard outer covering, as on eggs or clams. —*plural* **shells**

sher·iff (sher′ if) *noun*   the chief officer of the law in a county. —*plural* **sher′ iffs**

shin·y (shīn′ ē) *adjective*   bright; shining [The child found a *shiny* stone.] —**shin′ i·er, shin′ i·est**

shop·per (shöp′ ər) *noun*   one who shops. — *plural* **shop′ pers**

shorts (shôrts) *noun plural*   short pants that end above the knee.

should·n't (shood′ ′nt) should not

shout (shout) *verb*   to say in a loud voice [They *shouted* out the cheer.] —**shout′ ed, shout′ ing**

side·walk (sīd′ wôk) *noun*   a paved path for walking. —*plural* **side′ walks**

sigh (sī) *noun*   a long, noisy breath [The sad man gave a deep *sigh*.] —*plural* **sighs**

sight (sīt) *noun*   **1** something worth seeing [The Grand Canyon is a *sight* to remember.] —*plural* **sights 2** vision; eyesight [Glasses improved my *sight*.]

since (sins) *adverb*   from then until now [Lynn came Monday and has been here ever *since*.]

sip (sip) *verb* to drink a little at a time [She *sipped* the hot cocoa.] —**sipped, sip′ ping**

sis·ter (sis′ tər) *noun* a girl or woman as she is related to the other children of her parents. —*plural* **sis′ ters**

size (sīz) *noun* how large or how small a thing is [What *size* is this shirt?] —*plural* **siz′ es**

skat·er (skāt′ ər) *noun* a person who moves on ice skates or roller skates. —*plural* **skat′ ers**

skip (skip) *verb* to move by hopping on first one foot and then the other. —**skipped, skip′ ping**

slam (slam) *verb* to shut with force and noise [Please don't *slam* the door.] —**slammed, slam′ ming**

sleep·y (slēp′ ē) *adjective* drowsy. —**sleep′ i·er, sleep′ i·est**

slice (slīs) *verb* to cut into thin pieces [He *sliced* a loaf of bread.] —**sliced, slic′ ing**

slight (slīt) *adjective* not great or important [There will be a *slight* change in plans.]

small (smôl) *adjective* little in size [I'd like a *small* scoop of ice cream.] —**small′ er, small′ est**

smile (smīl) *verb* to show that one is pleased or happy by making the corners of the mouth turn up. —**smiled, smil′ ing**

smoke (smōk) *noun* the gas and bits of carbon that rise from something burning [*Smoke* rose from the campfire.]

smok·y (smō′ kē) *adjective* filled with smoke [The air looked gray in the *smoky* room.] —**smok′ i·er, smok′ i·est**

sniff (snif) *verb* to smell by pulling air through the nose [He *sniffed* the sour milk.] —**sniffed, sniff′ ing**

soak (sōk) *verb* to make wet by keeping in water [She *soaked* the sponge.] —**soaked, soak′ ing**

soap (sōp) *noun* a substance used with water to wash things.

some·one (sum′ wun) *pronoun* a certain person not named [*Someone* left the door open.]

some·times (sum′ tīmz) *adverb* occasionally [*Sometimes* we go to plays.]

sor·ry (sär′ ē) *adjective* full of sadness or pity [I'm *sorry* you got hurt.] —**sor′ri·er, sor′ri·est**

sound (sound) *noun* any noise that can be heard [I hear the *sound* of her footsteps.] —*plural* **sounds**

south (south) *noun* the direction to the left of a person facing the sunset.

spar·row (spar′ ō) *noun* a small gray and brown bird [A *sparrow* sang in the garden.] —*plural* **spar′rows**

speak (spēk) *verb* talk [They *spoke* to each other on the phone.] —**spoke, speak′ ing**

speak·er (spē′ kər) *noun* a person who speaks or makes speeches. —*plural* **speak′ ers**

spear (spir) *noun* weapon made of a long handle and a sharp point. —*plural* **spears**

spell (spel) *verb* to say or write in order the letters that make up a word [Can you *spell* "seize"?] —**spelled, spell′ ing**

spend (spend) *verb* to pay out or give up [He *spent* $50 for food.] —**spent, spend′ ing**

spin (spin) *verb* to whirl around swiftly [*Spin* the wheel.] —**spun, spin′ ning**

spin·ner (spin′ ər) *noun* a person, animal, or thing that spins [The spider is a *spinner* of webs.] —*plural* **spin′ ners**

a	fat	ir	here	ou	out	zh	leisure
ā	ape	ī	bite, fire	u	up	ng	ring
ä	car, lot	ō	go	ʉr	fur		a *in* ago
e	ten	ô	law, horn	ch	chin		e *in* agent
er	care	oi	oil	sh	she	ə =	i *in* unity
ē	even	oo	look	th	thin		o *in* collect
i	hit	o͞o	tool	th	then		u *in* focus

sport (spôrt) *noun* an active game for exercise or fun [Skiing is a winter *sport*.] —*plural* **sports**

spray (sprā) *verb* to shoot out in a mist of tiny drops [She *sprayed* water on the plants.] —**sprayed, spray' ing**

spy (spī) *noun* a person who watches others secretly [The *spy* peered through the window.] —*plural* **spies** ♦*verb* to act as a spy [Detectives *spied* on him.] —**spied, spy' ing**

squeak (skwēk) *noun* a short, high cry or sound [Do you hear the *squeak* of a mouse?] —*plural* **squeaks** ♦*verb* to make a squeak [His new shoes *squeaked*.] —**squeaked, squeak' ing**

squeak·y (skwēk' ē) *adjective* having a high sound. —**squeak' i·er, squeak' i·est**

squeeze (skwēz) *verb* to press hard [He *squeezed* the sponge dry.] —**squeezed, squeez' ing**

stack (stak) *verb* to arrange in a pile [The books were *stacked* on the table.] **stacked, stack' ing**

sta·ple (stā' p'l) *noun* a piece of metal driven into a surface to hold something in place. —*plural* **sta' ples** ♦*verb* to fasten with a staple or staples. —**sta' pled, sta' pling**

sta·pler (stā' plər) *noun* a device for driving staples. —*plural* **sta' plers**

star (stär) *noun* a heavenly body seen as a small point of light in the night sky. —*plural* **stars**

star·ry (stär'ē) *adjective* full of stars [Isn't there a *starry* sky tonight?] —**star' ri·er, star' ri·est**

stay (stā) *verb* remain. [*Stay* at home.] —**stayed, stay' ing**

steal (stēl) *verb* to take away something that does not belong to one. —**stole, stol' en, steal' ing**

step (step) *noun* a place to rest the foot in going up or down. —*plural* **steps**

still (stil) *adverb* until then or now [Is she *still* talking?]

sting (sting) *verb* to hurt by pricking [Bees can *sting* you.] —**stung, sting' ing**

stir (stʉr) *verb* to mix with a spoon or a fork [*Stir* the paint well.] —**stirred, stir' ring**

stone (stōn) *noun* rock [That monument is built of *stone*.] —*plural* **stones**

stop (stäp) *verb* to halt or keep from going on [*Stop* the car.] —**stopped, stop' ping**

storm (stôrm) *noun* a strong wind with rain, snow, or lightning [The *storm* knocked down the telephone lines.] —*plural* **storms**

sto·ry (stôr' ē) *noun* a telling of some true or made-up happening [Can you tell the *story* of the first Thanksgiving?] —*plural* **sto' ries**

stray (strā) *noun* a lost person or animal [We fed the *stray* some dog food.] —*plural* **strays** ♦*verb* to wander away [Don't *stray* from camp.] —**strayed, stray' ing**

stud·y (stud' ē) *verb* to read so as to understand and remember [*Study* your lessons.] —**stud' ied, stud' y·ing**

sub·way (sub' wā) *noun* an underground railway [He rode the *subway* downtown.] —*plural* **sub' ways**

sudden (sud' 'n) *adjective* not expected [A *sudden* storm came up.] —**sud' den·ly** *adverb*

suit·case (sōot' kās) *noun* a case for carrying belongings when traveling. —*plural* **suit' cas·es**

sum·mer (sum' ər) *noun* the warmest season of the year. —*plural* **sum' mers**

sun·ny (sun' ē) *adjective* bright with sunlight. —**sun' ni·er, sun' ni·est**

sup·per (sup' ər) *noun* the last meal of the day. —*plural* **sup' pers**

sup·pli·er (sə plī' ər) *noun* one who supplies. —*plural* **sup·pli' ers**

sup·ply (sə plī') *verb* to give what is needed [The camp *supplies* sheets and towels.] —**sup·plied', sup·ply'ing**

sur·vey (sur' vā) *noun* a general study [The *survey* shows that we need more schools.] —*plural* **sur' veys**

swal·low (swäl' ō) *verb* to let food or drink go through the throat to the stomach [She *swallowed* the peanut.] —**swal' lowed, swal' low·ing**

sway (swā) *verb* to swing or bend from side to side [Grass *swayed* in the wind.] —**swayed, sway' ing**

sweat·er (swet' ər) *noun* a knitted garment with sleeves. —*plural* **sweat' ers**

sweep (swēp) *verb* to clean by brushing with a broom [*Sweep* the floor.] —**swept, sweep' ing**

swim (swim) *verb* to move in water by using arms and legs [I love to *swim* in the lake.] —**swam, swum, swim' ming**

swim·mer (swim' ər) *noun* a person who swims. —*plural* **swim' mers**

T

tag (tag) *verb* to touch in the game of tag. —**tagged, tag' ging**

take (tāk) *verb* to get hold of; grasp [*Take* my hand as we cross the street.] —**took, tak' en, tak' ing**

talk (tôk) *verb* speak [The baby is learning to *talk*.] —**talked, talk' ing**

tame (tām) *adjective* no longer wild [Would you like a *tame* skunk?] —**tam'er, tam'est**

tear (ter) *verb* to rip or pull apart [*Tear* the paper into bits.] —**tore, torn, tear' ing**

tease (tēz) *verb* to bother [They *teased* my dog.] —**teased, teas' ing**

ten·nis (ten' is) *noun* a game in which players hit a ball back and forth over a net with rackets.

that's (*th*ats) that is.

them·selves (*th*em selvz') *pronoun* their own selves [They hurt *themselves*.]

there·fore (*th*er' fôr) *adverb* for this or that reason.

they'd (*th*ād) **1** they had. **2** they would.

thief (thēf) *noun* a person who steals. —*plural* **thieves**

thigh (thī) *noun* the part of the leg between the knee and hip. —*plural* **thighs**

think (thingk) to use the mind [*Think* before you act.] —**thought, think' ing**

thorn (thôrn) *noun* a sharp point growing out of a plant stem. —*plural* **thorns**

throat (thrōt) *noun* the upper part of the passage from the mouth to the stomach [I have a sore *throat*.] —*plural* **throats**

thumb (thum) *noun* the short, thick finger nearest the wrist. —*plural* **thumbs**

thun·der (thun' dər) *noun* the loud noise that comes after lightning.

tie (tī) *verb* to make a knot or bow [He *tied* his necktie.] —**tied, ty' ing**

tight (tīt) *adjective* fitting too closely [My shirt is too *tight*.] —**tight' er, tight' est**

tip (tip) *verb* to overturn; upset. —**tipped, tip' ping**

tire¹ (tīr) *noun* an air-filled rubber tube that fits around a wheel. —*plural* **tires**

tire² (tīr) *verb* exhaust [The hike *tired* me.] —**tired, tir' ing**

a	fat	ir	here	ou	out	zh	leisure
ā	ape	ī	bite, fire	u	up	ng	ring
ä	car, lot	ō	go	ur	fur		a *in* ago
e	ten	ô	law, horn	ch	chin		e *in* agent
er	care	oi	oil	sh	she	ə =	i *in* unity
ē	even	oo	look	th	thin		o *in* collect
i	hit	o͞o	tool	*th*	then		u *in* focus

toad (tōd) *noun* a small frog-like animal that lives on land. —*plural* **toads**

toast (tōst) *noun* bread that has been browned by heating.

to·mor·row (tə mär′ ō *or* tə môr′ ō) *noun* the day after today.

to·night (tə nīt′) *noun* this night.

tooth (to͞oth) *noun* white, bony part in the jaw used for biting and chewing. —*plural* **teeth**

tor·na·do (tôr nā′ dō) *noun* a funnel-shaped column of air that usually destroys everything in its path. —*plural* **tor·na′ does** *or* **tor·na′ dos**

toss (tôs) *verb* to throw easily [*Toss* the ball here.] —**tossed, toss′ ing**

toy (toi) *noun* a thing to play with. —*plural* **toys**

trace (trās) *verb* to copy a picture by following its lines on thin paper placed over it [She *traced* that drawing from a book.] —**traced, trac′ ing**

tray (trā) *noun* a flat piece of wood or metal for carrying food. —*plural* **trays**

trunk (trungk) *noun* a large, strong box for storing things or holding clothes while traveling [I packed my clothes in the *trunk*.] —*plural* **trunks**

try (trī) *verb* attempt [We must *try* to help him.] —**tried, try′ ing**

tur·key (tur′ kē) *noun* a large bird with a small head and spreading tail. —*plural* **tur′ keys**

tur·nip (tur′ nip) *noun* a plant with a round, white or yellow root that is eaten as a vegetable. —*plural* **tur′ nips**

twi·light (twī′ līt) *noun* the dim light just after sunset.

twin (twin) *noun* either of two born at the same time to the same mother [Bob and Betty are *twins*.] —*plural* **twins**

U

um·brel·la (um brel′ ə) *noun* cloth or plastic stretched over a frame at the top of a stick, used to protect one from the rain. —*plural* **um·brel′ las**

un·a·ble (un ā′b'l) *adjective* not having the power to do something [We were *unable* to push the car.]

un·a·fraid (un ə frād′) *adjective* not feeling fear.

un·bro·ken (un brō′ k'n) *adjective* not broken.

un·but·ton (un but′ 'n) *verb* to unfasten the buttons of. —**un·but′ toned, un·but′ ton·ing**

un·cle (uŋ′ k'l) *noun* the brother of one's father or mother. —*plural* **un′ cles**

un·cov·er (un kuv′ ər) *verb* to remove the cover from [*Uncover* the bird cage.] —**un·cov′ ered, un·cov′ er·ing**

un·der (un′ dər) *preposition* in a lower position; below [It rolled *under* the table.]

un·der·stand (un dər stand′) *verb* to get the meaning of [Do you *understand* my question?] —**un·der·stood′, un·der·stand′ ing**

un·e·qual (un ē′ kwəl) *adjective* not equal [We were given *unequal* shares.]

un·e·ven (un ē′ vən) *adjective* not even [Be careful on the *uneven* ground.]

un·fair (un fer′) *adjective* not fair or honest [The umpire's call was *unfair*.]

un·fas·ten (un fas′ 'n) *verb* untie; open, etc. —**un·fas′ tened, un·fas′ ten·ing**

un·health·y (un hel′ thē) *adjective* not well; sick. —**un·health′ i·er, un·health′ i·est**

un·hurt (un hurt′) *adjective* not having pain, injury, or harm [She came out of the burning building *unhurt*.]

un·kind (un kīnd′) *adjective* not kind; hurting the feelings of others [Those *unkind* words made him sad.]

un·less (ən les′) *conjunction* except if [I won't go *unless* you do.]

un·lock (un läk′) *verb* to open by undoing a lock [This key won't *unlock* the door.] —**un·locked′, un·lock′ ing**

un·o·pened (un ō′ p'nd) *adjective* closed or covered [What was behind the *unopened* door?]

un·pack (un pak′) *verb* to open and empty out [I'll *unpack* the suitcase.] —**un·packed′, un·pack· ing**

un·plug (un plug′) *verb* to remove a plug. —**un·plugged′, un·plug′ ging**

un·ripe (un rīp′) *adjective* not ripe [Don't eat the *unripe* fruit.]

un·safe (un sāf′) *adjective* not safe; dangerous [That shaky ladder is *unsafe*.]

un·tie (un tī′) *verb* to unfasten something that is tied. —**un·tied′, un·ty′ ing**

un·true (un trōō′) *adjective* not correct; false [What he said was *untrue*.]

un·will·ing (un wil′ ing) *adjective* not willing or ready [He is *unwilling* to take the blame.]

un·wise (un wīz′) *adjective* not showing good sense [It's *unwise* to skate without knee pads.]

un·wrap (un rap′) *verb* to open by taking off the wrapping. —**un·wrapped′, un·wrap′ ping**

up·stairs (up′ sterz′) *adverb* to or on an upper floor [Let's go *upstairs*.]

use (yōōz) *verb* to put into action [He *used* the vacuum cleaner.] —**used, us′ ing**

V

val·ley (val′ ē) *noun* low land between hills or mountains. —*plural* **val′ leys**

vase (vās *or* vāz) *noun* a container for holding flowers. —*plural* **vas′ es**

ver·y (ver′ ē) *adverb* extremely [It is *very* cold.]

view (vyōō) *noun* scene [We admired the *view* from the bridge.] —*plural* **views**

W

wade (wād) *verb* to walk through water, mud, or anything that slows one down. —**wad′ ed, wad′ ing**

wag (wag) *verb* to move quickly back and forth [The dog *wagged* its tail.] —**wagged, wag′ ging**

wag·on (wag′ən) *noun* a four-wheeled vehicle for carrying heavy loads [Two horses pulled the *wagon*.] —*plural* **wag′ ons**

wake (wāk) *verb* awake [*Wake* up!] —**woke, wak′ ing**

walk (wôk) *verb* to move along on foot [*Walk*, do not run, to the nearest exit.] **walked, walk′ ing**

warm (wôrm) *adjective* having or feeling a little heat; not cool but not hot [I was too *warm*, so I took off my sweater.]

warn (wôrn) *verb* to tell of danger [The lighthouse beamed a signal to *warn* ships.] —**warned, warn′ ing**

was·n't (wuz′ 'nt) was not.

watch (wäch *or* wôch) *verb* to look at [They *watched* the parade.] —**watched, watch′ ing**

water (wôt′ ər) *noun* the liquid that falls as rain and is found in lakes, rivers, and oceans.

a	fat	ir	here	ou	out	zh	leisure
ā	ape	ī	bite, fire	u	up	ng	ring
ä	car, lot	ō	go	ur	fur		a *in* ago
e	ten	ô	law, horn	ch	chin		e *in* agent
er	care	oi	oil	sh	she	ə =	i *in* unity
ē	even	oo	look	th	thin		o *in* collect
i	hit	ōō	tool	th	then		u *in* focus

wave (wāv) *verb*   to move back and forth [The toddler *waved* his hand.] —**waved, wav′ ing**

wear (wer) *verb*   to have on the body [Do you *wear* glasses?] —**wore, worn, wear′ ing**

weath·er (weth′ ər) *noun*   the conditions outside relating to temperature, sunshine, etc. [We have good *weather* today for a picnic.]

we'd (wēd)   **1** we had.   **2** we should.   **3** we would.

week·end (wēk′ end′) *noun*   the time from Friday night to Monday morning. —*plural* **week′ ends′**

we'll (wēl) we will.

we're (wir) we are.

weren't (wʉrnt) were not.

wet (wet) *adjective*   covered or soaked with liquid [Wipe it off with a *wet* rag.] —**wet′ ter, wet′ test**

what's (hwuts) what is.

who's (ho̅o̅z) who is, who has.

wide (wīd) *adjective*   measuring a lot from side to side [The trailer was very *wide*.] —**wid′ er, wid′ est**

wife (wīf) *noun*   a married woman. —*plural* **wives**

wig·gle (wig′ 'l) *verb*   to twist from side to side [The polliwog moves by *wiggling* its tail.] —**wig′ gled, wig′ gling**

will·ing (wil′ ing) *adjective*   agreeing to do something [Are you *willing* to try?]

win (win) *verb*   to get the victory in a contest [I might *win* the spelling bee.] —**won, win′ ning**

wind·y (win′ dē) *adjective*   with much wind [It's a *windy* day.] —**wind′ i·er, wind′ i·est**

win·ner (win′ ər) *noun*   one that wins a contest or race [The *winner* of the election will be president.] —*plural* **win′ ners**

win·ter (win′ tər) *noun*   the coldest season of the year. —*plural* **win′ ters**

wip·er (wīp′ ər) *noun*   one who wipes. —*plural* **wip′ ers**

wish (wish) *noun*   something wanted or hoped for [He got his *wish*.] —*plural* **wish′ es**

wolf (woolf) *noun*   a wild animal that looks like a dog. —*plural* **wolves**

wom·an (wo̅o̅m′ ən) *noun*   an adult female human being. —*plural* **wom′ en**

wool·en (wool′ ən) *adjective*   made of wool [He wore a heavy *woolen* jacket.]

word (wʉrd) *noun*   a sound or group of sounds having meaning and used as a single unit of speech. —*plural* **words**

work·er (wʉr′ kər) *noun*   a person who works. —*plural* **work·ers**

world (wʉrld) *noun*   the earth or a planet thought of as like the earth [Magellan's crew sailed around the *world*.] —*plural* **worlds**

worm (wʉrm) *noun*   a small, creeping animal with a soft, thin body and no legs. —*plural* **worms**

wor·ry (wʉr′ ē) *verb*   to be or make troubled in mind [She *worried* about her grades.] —**wor′ ried, wor′ ry·ing**

worst (wʉrst) *adjective*   most evil.

worth (wʉrth) *adjective*   equal in value to [It's not *worth* a nickel.]

wrap·per (rap′ ər) *noun*   a covering [Our newspaper is mailed in a paper *wrapper*.] —*plural* **wrap′ pers**

wreck (rek) *verb*   to destroy or ruin [The car was *wrecked* in an accident.] —**wrecked, wreck′ ing**

wren (ren) *noun*   a small songbird. —*plural* **wrens**

wrench (rench) *noun*　a tool for holding and turning nuts and bolts. —*plural* **wrench′ es**

wrin·kle (ring′ k'l) *noun*　a small or uneven fold [Can you iron the *wrinkles* from this shirt?] —*plural* **wrink′ les**

wrist (rist) *noun*　the part of the arm between the hand and forearm. —*plural* **wrists**

write (rīt) *verb*　to be the author of [Dickens *wrote* novels.] —**wrote, writ′ ing**

wrong (rông) *adjective*　not the one that is correct or wanted [That is the *wrong* door.] ♦ *adverb* incorrectly [You answered the question *wrong*.]

Y

year (yir) *noun*　a period of 365 days. —*plural* **years**

yes·ter·day (yes′ tər dē *or* yes′ tər dā) *noun*　the day before today.

you'd (yo͞od)　**1** you had.　**2** you would.

young (yung) *adjective*　not old [That *young* boy is very talkative.] —**young′ er, young′ est**

your·self (yər self′) *pronoun*　your own self [Did you cut *yourself*?] —*plural* **your·selves′**

you've (yo͞ov) you have.

Z

zip·per (zip′ ər) *noun*　a device used to fasten two edges of cloth [His coat *zipper* is stuck.] —*plural* **zip′ pers**

a	fat	**ir**	here	**ou**	out	**zh**	leisure
ā	ape	**ī**	bite, fire	**u**	up	**ng**	ring
ä	car, lot	**ō**	go	**ʉr**	fur		a *in* ago
e	ten	**ô**	law, horn	**ch**	chin		e *in* agent
er	care	**oi**	oil	**sh**	she	**ə** =	i *in* unity
ē	even	**oo**	look	**th**	thin		o *in* collect
i	hit	**o͞o**	tool	**th**	then		u *in* focus

Handwriting Practice

Lesson 2

oa

boat
float
goat

Lesson 5

ys

cowboys
plays
trays
keys

Lesson 4

xes

boxes
foxes

Lesson 11

bb

ribbon

yed

stayed
obeyed
sprayed
played

gg

wagged
begged
bragged

wr

wrote

or

fork
short
world
story

er

river
every
summer

ear

wear
earth
year

dy

windy
shady
muddy

igh

flight
high
light

mb

comb
crumb
lamb
climb

ve

I've,
you've

tt

little
bottle
rattle
cattle

ck

unlucky
unlock
unpack

a b c d e f g h i j k l m n

o p q r s t u v w x y z

A B C D E F G H I J K L

M N O P Q R S T U V

W X Y Z

a b c d e f g h i j

k l m n o p q r s

t u v w x y z

A B C D E F G H I

J K L M N O P Q R

S T U V W X Y Z

ILLUSTRATIONS
David Cunningham: 5
Gwen Connolly: 7, 8, 12, 17, 32, 38, 40, 59, 63, 73, 82, 84, 85,
86, 87, 109, 115, 124, 154, 155, 161, 164, 168, 170, 171, 173, 174,
175, 177, 180
Edward Aitchinson: 9, 11, 14, 15, 16, 19, 20, 21, 24, 25, 29, 30,
31, 34, 44, 46
B. J. Johnson: 13, 18, 23, 28, 33, 34, 43
Paul Vaccarello: 22, 27, 37, 42, 68, 88, 104, 129, 150
Carol Stutz: 24, 34, 37, 39
Martucci Studio/Jerry Malone: 52, 98, 144
Andrea Eberbach: 54, 64, 69, 74, 79, 89, 231, 232
Joe Veno: 55, 56, 57, 60, 61, 62, 65, 66, 67, 70, 71, 72, 75, 77,
80, 83, 90, 92
Dick Martin: 100, 105, 110, 120, 125, 130, 135
Larry Frederick: 101, 102, 103, 106, 107, 108, 111, 112, 113, 118,
121, 122, 123, 126, 127, 128, 131, 132, 133, 134, 136, 138, 199,
201, 202, 204, 205, 206, 208, 209, 211, 212, 213, 214, 216, 218,
221, 222, 224, 225
Tani Johnson: 146, 151, 156, 166, 176, 181
Slug Signorino: 147, 148, 149, 152, 153, 157, 158, 159, 163, 167,
169, 178, 179, 182, 184

Cover Photograph: Jeanne White/Photo Researchers
Cover Design: Martucci Studio

Editorial Credits

Executive Editor, Language Arts: Carolyn McConnell

Senior Editor: Sandra Corniels

Associate Editors: Lisa Maria DeSloover, Patricia
King, Carol Kalas McMullen

Project Assistance: Brown Publishing Network, Inc.

Art and Design: Chestnut House, Martucci Studio

Acknowledgments
Marian Reiner: For "Secret Talk" from *A Word or Two with You* by Eve Merriam; copyright © 1981 by Eve Merriam, all rights
reserved. Marian Reiner: for "Think of Tree" from *I Thought I Heard the City* by Lilian Moore; copyright © 1969 by Lilian
Moore, all rights reserved.